SCHOLASTIC

A Poem for Every Day!

BY SUSAN MOGER

NEW YORK • TORONTO • LONDON • AUCKLAND • SYDNEY
MEXICO CITY • NEW DELHI • HONG KONG • BUENOS AIRES

Teaching Resources

For Patricia
Sister, Poet

ACKNOWLEDGMENTS

A very early memory of mine is listening to my parents, Roy and Charlotte Moger, sing patriotic songs as they cleaned our house together. Thanks to their love of stories, songs, and poems I grew up knowing that playing with words is a wise use of time.

Thanks to Sid Reischer, the pages of this book are enlivened by the work of his talented fourth- and fifth-grade students. Thanks to all of you! And to others who shared poems and ideas about teaching poetry—Patricia Moger, Rachel and Roy Moger-Reischer, Margret Kingrey, Shirley Johannesen Levine, and Carol Peck. Thanks to my husband Ted and son Ben for their love and encouragement.

I'd also like to acknowledge three people who long ago introduced me to poets who have held me captive ever since: Elizabeth Moger, who shared T. S. Eliot and Elinor Wylie with me and convinced me to go to a Jean Redpath concert where I heard "Song of Wandering Aengus" by William Butler Yeats; Alf Hiltebeitel who played me a recording of Dylan Thomas reading "Fern Hill"; and Reg Hannaford who introduced me to James Joyce.

Terry Cooper and Virginia Dooley at Scholastic Teaching Resources entrusted this wonderful project to me, and Kathy Massaro gave it form and shape and made it real.

Thank you all!

CREDITS AND PERMISSIONS

"We Are a Living People." Reprinted by permission of Lori Wautier. "For everyone of the Native Culture."

"Spelling Bee" by David McCord. From TAKE SKY by David TW McCord Trust. Copyright © 1962 by David McCord. By permission of Little, Brown and Co., Inc.

"This is Not the Moon" by Ariwara No Norihara, "A Wild Sea" by Basho, and "The Cicada Sings" translated by Kenneth Roxroth. From ONE HUNDRED POEMS FROM THE JAPANESE translated by Kennth Rexroth. Copyright © 1955 by New Directions Publishing Corp. Reprinted by permission of New Directions Publishing Corp. All rights reserved.

"You . . . and Your Dad" by Katie Ferman, age 11, is reprinted with permission from STONE SOUP, the magazine by young writers and artists. Copyright © 2004 by the Children's Art Foundation.

(continued on inside back cover)

Cover design by Jaime Lucero
Interior design by Kathy Massaro
Interior illustrations by James Graham Hale

ISBN: 0-439-65613-3

Copyright © 2006 by Susan Moger. All rights reserved. Printed in the U.S.A.

5 6 7 8 9 10   40   14 13 12 11 10 09 08 07 06

Table of Contents

Haiku
page 60

Poems About People, Places, and Things
page 62

Poems About Poetry and Words

page 91

Introduction

Poetry throws open the windows and rolls up the rugs—
Put on your poetry shoes and dance!

Poetry matters. Poetry enriches, enlivens, and informs. The best poetry aligns us differently with the world and ourselves.

The poems collected in this book have been chosen for you to use throughout the school year. You'll find poems that delight and poems that demand attention. Poems that speak of what it is to be an American and what it is to be a part of the living world. There are classic poems; poems by lesser-known poets, old and new; and poems by very young poets. There are serious poems, provocative poems, and poems for fun. Every poem, long or short, has something to teach: about the way words can speed you along or pull you up short, about rhymes and rhythms, and about images that speak to us across time.

In the following sections you'll find ideas for memorizing poems, using poems as models for students' poetry, illustrating poems, and reading poems aloud. There are also ideas for connecting the poems with topics in the curriculum and for sharing poems with students' families. Best of all, you'll find the poems a source of endless delight for you and your students. Poems in the classroom are like seeds: scatter them widely and often and see what grows—students' appreciation of language, new ways of seeing, enjoyment of writing. Never underestimate the power of a poem to change a person's life.

Enjoy them all!

A Poem for Every Day: Why?

Hearing a poem every day, especially well-written, contemporary poems that students do not have to analyze, . . . [can] convince students that poetry can be an understandable, painless and even eye-opening part of their everyday experience.

—Library of Congress

However you choose to use the poems in this book, consider reading, or having students read, at least one poem each day for the entire school year. (The collection contains more than 180 poems, so you can choose which ones suit your class best and sometimes even splurge on two a day.)

A Poem for Every Day: How?

◎ Start or end the school day (or class period) with a poem you, or one or more students, read aloud. Long poems like "Paul Revere's Ride" (12), "Barbara Frietchie" (13), or "Casey at the Bat" (173) can be spread out and savored over many days. Several students can participate in reading aloud these long poems. Consider distributing copies of a long poem on the day you plan to start reading it, so that by the time students hear the end read aloud, a few days later, they will be familiar with the entire poem.

◎ During National Poetry Month (April), arrange for your students to use the PA system to read a poem at the start (or end) of each school day. During the rest of the year, if possible, read a school-wide poem at the beginning of each week. Choose from the poems in this book, your students' poems, or other favorite poems.

◎ Make the case for reading poetry every day with information you'll find online about the Library of Congress's Project 180. This national initiative for high school students is described on the Project 180 Web site (see the Resources section on page 14).

About This Book

In this book you'll find classic poems by famous poets and brand-new poems by emerging poets, many of whom were in fourth or fifth grade when they wrote their poems included here. The poems in the collection can be read aloud (by one or more readers) or savored silently. They can be used as springboards for writing, for explorations of meaning, and for analyses of form (such as haiku or cinquain) rhyme and rhythm, and imagery, personification, and alliteration.

The poems are organized in the following categories:

- **Poems for Patriots**
- **Poems About the Living World**
- **Haiku**
- **Poems About People, Places, and Things**
- **Poems About Poetry and Words**
- **Poems of Beauty and Magic**
- **Poems for Fun**

The following information appears immediately following many of the poems. Some poems appear without comment; just read them and enjoy.

Vocabulary Key: Archaic and difficult words that occur in a poem are highlighted in the body of the poem and defined in this section.

Links: This section offers suggestions for linking a poem with others on similar topics—for example, "The Bells" (149) and "The Bells of Shandon" (151); to others by the same poet; or to poems with similar rhymes, rhythms, or imagery.

Springboard: Discussion questions and activities are provided in this section.

Find Out More: In this section you'll find suggestions for further explorations about the poet or the poem.

Sharing the Poems

◎ Read the poems in this book aloud to your students. Make photocopies of the poem available to students so they can follow along as you read aloud. Invite them to take turns reading aloud from the book as well (see the Reading Aloud section on page 10).

◎ Photocopy poems you like or poems on the same topic (see Connections Chart, page 16), and then do one or more of the following:

   ✳ place copies of poems in a folder in your literature resource center;
   ✳ post the copies on a bulletin board;
   ✳ distribute copies to students to read and discuss.

◎ Make this book available to students so they can copy out short poems into their notebooks. Make sure they understand they must include the title, author's name, and poem number when they do this.

◎ Make audio- or videotapes of students reading poetry aloud.

◎ Talk about the poems you read. Ask students what they liked or didn't like on first hearing or reading a poem. Revisit the poem and see if students' reactions have changed. Talk about how poems are different from each other and from prose.

◎ Some of the poems are songs—invite someone who plays an instrument to bring in music and play for you to sing along.

Ideas for Extending *A Poem for Every Day!*

Poetry Notebooks

Introduce the poetry notebook at the beginning of the school year. Explain that you will be keeping a poetry notebook along with the class and that the notebook is dedicated to poetry. Below is a list of uses for the poetry notebook. From time to time, discuss students' ideas for other uses for the notebooks and how to share their contents.

How to Read a Poem Out Loud

Billy Collins

Former Poet Laureate of the United States

1. Read the poem slowly. . . . [This] will not just make the poem easier to hear; it will underscore the importance in poetry of each and every word. A poem cannot be read too slowly, and a good way for a reader to set an easy pace is to pause for a few seconds between the title and the poem's first line.

2. Read in a normal, relaxed tone of voice. . . . Let the words of the poem do the work. Just speak clearly and slowly.

3. Obviously, poems come in lines, but pausing at the end of every line will create a choppy effect and interrupt the flow of the poem's sense. Readers should pause only where there is punctuation, just as you would when reading prose, only more slowly.

4. Use a dictionary to look up unfamiliar words and hard-to-pronounce words. . . . [You] might want to write out a word phonetically as a reminder of how it should sound. It should be emphasized that learning to read a poem out loud is a way of coming to a full understanding of that poem, perhaps a better way than writing a paper on the subject.

Use your poetry notebook to:

*   respond to poems you read.

*   write ideas for poems (quick word "snapshots" that later can be developed into poems).

*   list rhyming words; interesting words; old-fashioned "poetic" words; and words from the Vocabulary Key definitions in this book.

*   encourage students to date their entries. Collect the poetry journals periodically, but only to gauge a student's level of engagement with the task, not to critique the contents.

Reading Aloud

*   Most of the poems in this collection lend themselves to being read aloud. You can model reading aloud effectively (see Billy Collins' suggestions, left) and then invite individual students to read poems aloud, alone or as part of a group. Long poems can be shared among many readers.

*   A list of poems in this collection that are particularly appropriate for reading aloud, by one, two, or more readers, is provided in the Connections Chart on page 16 (as a topic under Language Arts).

*   After students have written poetry individually, invite teams of students to create poems for three or more voices. The poem might have a chorus with different stanzas on the same topic from different perspectives. Present a poetry reading to other classes; tape-record or videotape the presentation and donate it to the school library.

Memorizing Poems

66 . . . [T]he beauty of a poem, once learned, is not in the recitation of words. The poem, committed to memory, becomes a vehicle of communion for the self and the soul. 99

—Henry H. Emurian

Memorizing a poem, or, in the old-fashioned phrase, "getting a poem by heart," has gone out of style in today's classrooms, but students today are just as capable of memorizing as their great-grandparents were. They memorize all sorts of things—sports facts, jokes, song lyrics, details about the lives of pop stars, and the myriad cell phone numbers, email addresses, and personal preferences of their friends and family members.

There are many good reasons to ask students to memorize poetry. Probably the best reason is that "getting a poem by heart," makes it yours in a unique way. Memorizing a poem builds self-confidence. Being able to recall a poem weeks or even months later is tremendously satisfying.

You can model the assignment by memorizing a short poem in this collection. Once you have memorized it, ask students to "test" your recall and then challenge them to memorize a poem they like. Follow the steps below and have students practice with a partner until both have learned their poems "by heart." Then have a Poetry Recital. Share the hints for memorizing a poem (right) with students.

Reading Poetry Across the Curriculum

◉ Review the Connections Chart on page 16 to see how poems in this collection complement topics in language arts, social studies, and science.

◉ Consider reading relevant poems aloud or photocopying and displaying them when your class is working on a particular topic.

Family Connections

From the beginning of the school year, encourage students to share poetry with their families.

Poetry Celebration

◉ After students have read aloud, written, and memorized poems, invite families to come to an in-class celebration of poetry. In the invitation, encourage family members to bring along a favorite poem to share.

◉ In a special corner of the classroom, display poems written by students, copies of poems from this collection, and other books of poetry. Consider creating a bulletin board devoted to poetry from many cultures.

Hints for Memorizing a Poem

⟆ Break the poem into parts and memorize a few lines (or a whole stanza) at a time. Visualize what the poet is saying and speak the words out loud. Read and then try to remember what you read (turn away from the page or close your eyes). Repeat this process until you can recite out loud the entire first section or stanza. Don't move on until you can do this.

⟆ Repeat the process for each section separately. As you finish a section, try linking it to the ones that came before. That way you'll have a complete poem by the time you're done.

⟆ Put your brain to work while you're sleeping! Read the poem over right before you turn out the light to go to sleep.

⟆ Test yourself by reciting the poem to your partner. This will help you figure out what places you need to work on.

⟆ Recite the poem to an audience of family and friends and/or classmates.

⟆ Bask in your accomplishment, but check back periodically (weekly, monthly) to make sure you are keeping the poem "in mind."

◎ During the celebration:

❋ Read a favorite poem and briefly explain why it is meaningful to you.

❋ Invite students to read poems they like and poems they have written and to recite poems they have memorized.

The Gift of Poetry

Students can give their poems as gifts to parents, grandparents, and other special people in their lives. They can decorate, laminate, and/or frame a single poem or print out, illustrate, and bind a collection of several poems.

Poetry Activities

Starter Activity: Forming the Poetry Habit

◎ The point of this first week's activity is to get in the habit of hearing a poem every day and responding to it, in discussion and in writing.

◎ On a Monday (of the first full week of school or at another good starting point) choose five poems from this collection, one for each day of the week, and make copies to distribute to students, one each day. Read aloud one poem a day to the class.

◎ After each reading have a short discussion to clarify anything students did not understand and to collect personal responses to the poems. This is the time to introduce Poetry Notebooks.

◎ Invite students to choose a word or phrase they like from the poems and "capture" it in their Poetry Notebook.

Writing Poetry: Understanding Forms

Once students become accustomed to hearing poems and responding to them, the next step is to write their own. The poems in this collection by young poets are listed in the Connections Chart on page 16 under Language Arts. Like all the poems in the collection, they can serve as models and inspiration.

Two-Word Line Poems

A great way to start poetry writing is to have students create poems with two-word lines. The simplicity is appealing—the lines can rhyme or not; the poem can be long or short. Any topic is welcomed. For example,

My teacher
always helpful
loves music
welcomes discussion
reads aloud

Name Poems

Name poems describe a person, in single words or whole sentences. The challenge is to start each line with a word that corresponds to a letter in a person's name so that when the poem is finished and read from top to bottom, the first letter of each line spells the person's name.

Example:

ROY
R eally fun to talk to.
O what a ballplayer!
Y es, he's a poet, too.

Other examples in this collection are "Tiger" (38), "Whales" (40), and "Nubian Goats"(43).

Color, Taste, "How Many Ways to Say . . ." Poems

This collection includes some remarkable color poems by students. Other senses can be tapped for inspiration too—see, for example, "Fried Dough" (121). The format "How Many Ways to Say . . ." is good for generating words and phrases that later can be developed into a poem in another format. "How Many Ways to Say Cooking?" (120) is an excellent example of this type of poem. A good example of a color poem is "Yellow" (156).

Haiku and Senryu

Haiku and senryu are short but very expressive poetic forms that your students will enjoy writing. Haiku and senryu pack lots of meaning into just 17 unrhymed syllables in three lines of poetry—5 syllables in the first line, 7 syllables in the second line, and 5 in the last line. Formal Japanese haiku are about nature and most contain a season word, either spring, fall, winter, or summer or a concrete image that represents a season, for example, nightingale, plum branch, moonlight. Senryu follows the same format as haiku but imposes no limitations on subject matter.

Despite their short length, haiku and senryu are divided into two parts; in English the dividing line is between the second and third lines. Both sections must enrich the understanding of the other. For examples of classroom haiku as well as some by Japanese poets, see the Haiku section of this collection (poems 66–75).

Cinquain

A cinquain is a five-line poem. The name of the form comes from the French word meaning "five." Usually a cinquain follows this format:

Line 1: a noun

Line 2: two adjectives describing the noun on Line 1

Line 3: three words ending with *-ing* (action words) that describe the noun on Line 1

Line 4: a phrase expressing a feeling usually about the noun on Line 1

Line 5: a synonym of the word on Line 1, or a word that sums up the poem

A cinquain also can be written to a syllable-count as follows:

Line 1: two syllables (subject or title)

Line 2: four syllables that describe Line 1

Line 3: six syllables expressing action that relate to Line 1

Line 4: eight syllables expressing a feeling

Line 5: a two-syllable synonym of the word in Line 1

Here is an example of a cinquain following this format:

Tigers
wild, beautiful
climbing, pacing, sleeping
dream of freedom—life beyond fences
Captives

For examples of cinquains composed by students, see "The American Flag" (2), "Insects" (34), and "Brother in Hospital" (88). "Brother in Hospital" has a more loosely interpreted format but is very effective.

Writing Poetry Across the Curriculum

◎ Encourage students to write poems about what they are learning in social studies, science, and math. A simple poem that contrasts two states of mind, such as "I used to [think, believe, wonder] . . . but now I [know, realize, understand] . . ." or "How Many Ways to Say . . ." can help reinforce students' learning. For example, in social studies:

I used to think Columbus discovered America.
But now I know more about the people who were living here when he arrived.

Or in earth science:

> **I used to imagine** that islands floated on the surface of the ocean.
> **But now I know** they are the tops of underwater mountains.

◎ After completing a unit in social studies, science, or math, use this format to write a class poem, with students contributing to a list of "How Many Ways to Say . . ." statements.

◎ Have students use similes and metaphors to describe social studies events, science concepts, or math processes. SOCIAL STUDIES: British taxation of the colonies was *like a hand* reaching across the ocean to take money to use far away. SCIENCE: Lava flows *like a river of fire*. MATH: Estimating is *like a tame version of a wild guess*.

Here are some other ideas for using poetry in specific subjects:

Math

When writing poetry in the form of haiku, senryu, or cinquain (see pages 13–14) students have to count syllables and add them up—a union of math and poetry skills.

Social Studies and Science

Writing name poems (see poems 38, 40, and 43) about people or concepts can help students check their understanding and increase vocabulary. A class set of name poems on LINCOLN (focusing on the qualities that made him great) could result in a nuanced biographical portrait of the 16th president of the United States. Haiku is typically about nature or the seasons and ties in nicely with science topics. (See the Connections Chart on page 16.)

Art

Post several poems that lend themselves to illustration, such as "Red, White, and Blue" (7), "Adowe" (21), "The Eagle" (32), or "On the Mississippi" (46). Invite students to work individually to illustrate a poem of their choosing. Display the illustrations and discuss the different visions the poems inspired. Encourage students to illustrate a poem they wrote themselves.

Drama

Invite students to work in groups to act out a poem or part of a poem, such as "Our Clever Hands" (112), "Last Leaf" (41), or, for the ambitious, "Paul Revere's Ride" (12).

Language Arts

Invite students to write poems for kindergarten or first-grade students. They can print out the poems, illustrate them, make copies, and take the anthology to read and present to a class of younger students.

Resources
(continued)

Poetry Books

Helen Ferris, *Favorite Poems Old and New*, Doubleday, 1957.

Paul Fleischman, *I Am Phoenix: Poems for Two Voices*, HarperTrophy, 1989.

__ *Big Talk: Poems for Four Voices*, Candlewick Press, 2000.

Donald Hall, Ed., *The Oxford Illustrated Book of American Children's Poems*, Oxford University Press, 1999.

Langston Hughes, *The Dream Keeper and Other Poems*, Knopf, 1996.

Rosemary Alexander, Ed., *Poetry Place Anthology*, Scholastic, 1983.

Edward Lear, *The Pelican Chorus: and Other Nonsense*, HarperTrophy, 2004.

Deborah Slier, Ed., *Make a Joyful Sound: Poems for Children by African-American Poets*, Checkerboard Press, 1991.

Connections Chart

Language Arts		Social Studies		Science	
Topic	**Poem Number**	**Topic**	**Poem Number**	**Topic**	**Poem Number**
Narrative Poems	12, 13, 141, 160, 167, 172, 186	Patriotic Songs and Symbols	1, 2, 4, 5, 8, 9, 10, 13, 14, 15, 16, 17	Living World	21, 29, 42, 148
Classic Poems and Poets	1, 3, 4, 5, 10, 12, 13, 14, 15, 22, 25, 26, 27, 28, 29, 32, 36, 44, 46, 47, 48, 49, 52, 61, 62, 63, 76, 79, 82, 83, 91, 100, 101, 102, 105, 109, 110, 111, 115, 117, 127, 131, 137, 138, 139, 140, 141, 144, 147, 148, 149, 151, 152, 158, 159, 160, 161, 163, 166, 167, 168, 169, 173, 174, 177, 179, 183, 184, 185, 186	American People	3, 6, 8, 10, 11, 12, 13, 17, 18, 19, 20, 78, 82	Animals and Birds	23, 25, 26, 27, 28, 30, 31, 32, 33, 34, 35, 36, 38, 39, 40, 43, 48, 51, 58, 62, 145, 165, 166
		American Revolution and War of 1812	1, 12, 14	Flowers and Trees	37, 41, 44, 56, 58, 60, 148
Relationship Poems	81, 82, 83, 84, 86, 87, 88, 89, 90, 91, 92, 141, 142	Civil War	9, 13, 18, 19, 20	Seasons	22, 24, 41, 50, 51, 57, 59, 66, 67, 71, 73, 75, 95, 97, 102, 138, 148, 150, 154, 158, 159
Read-Aloud Poems for One or More Voices (Partial List)	2, 12, 13, 21, 41, 47, 48, 55, 62, 76, 78, 81, 93, 102, 103, 104, 105, 106, 114, 115, 117, 119, 121, 123, 128, 130, 137, 138, 139, 141, 145, 149, 150, 151, 158, 160, 162, 164, 165, 166, 167, 169, 170, 173, 184, 185, 186	Technology	49, 103, 105	Water and Ocean	45, 46, 47, 48, 63, 64, 65, 70, 110, 140, 153, 154, 159, 164
Personification (Partial List)	98, 101, 105, 107, 113, 132, 152				
Imagery (Partial List)	52, 62, 86, 87, 101, 111, 117, 121, 128, 155, 156, 157	African-American Poets	9, 10, 18, 19, 22, 24, 33, 95, 101, 132	Weather and Wind	22, 52, 54, 55, 73, 161, 186
Poems by Young Poets	2, 7, 16, 34, 38, 40, 43, 51, 64, 65, 66, 67, 68, 72, 73, 74, 78, 81, 84, 88, 90, 96, 97, 107, 114, 120, 121, 146, 154, 155, 156, 157	Native American Poets	6, 17, 21, 106	Sun, Moon, and Stars	61, 62, 137, 152
Haiku	66–75				

Poems For Patriots

1

The Star-Spangled Banner (Excerpt)

O say, can you see, by the dawn's early light,
What so proudly we hailed at the twilight's last gleaming?
Whose broad stripes and bright stars, through the **perilous** fight,
O'er the **ramparts** we watched, were so **gallantly** streaming!

And the rockets' red glare, the bombs bursting in air,
Gave proof through the night that our flag was still there:

O say, does that star-spangled banner yet wave
O'er the land of the free and the home of the brave?

—Francis Scott Key

Key Vocabulary

perilous: dangerous
ramparts: walls of a fort
gallantly: bravely

Links

"The American Flag" (2),
"Barbara Frietchie" (13)

2

The American Flag

Freedom
Blowing, Moving
Red, White, Blue, Stars and Stripes
Waving so beautiful and proud
Our Flag

—Rebecca Godfrey, 5th grader, 2002

Links

"The Star-Spangled Banner" (1),
"Red, White, and Blue" (7), "Insects" (34),
"Brother in Hospital" (88)

Springboard

Discuss the cinquain form (see page 14)
and challenge students to use it to write
poems about the flag or other symbols of
America.

3 | I Hear America Singing

I hear America singing, the varied **carols** I hear,

Those of mechanics, each one singing his, as it should be, **blithe** and strong;

The carpenter singing his, as he measures his plank or beam,

The mason singing his, as he makes ready for work, or leaves off work,

The boatman singing what belongs to him in his boat—the deckhand singing on
      the steamboat deck;

The shoemaker singing as he sits on his bench, the **hatter** singing as he stands,

The wood-cutter's song, the ploughboy's on his way in the morning, or at the
      noon intermission, or at sundown;

The delicious singing of the mother, or of the young wife at work, or of the girl
      sewing or washing,

Each singing what belongs to her, and to none else,

The day what belongs to the day—at night, the party of young fellows, robust,
      friendly,

Singing with open mouths their strong melodious songs.

—Walt Whitman

Key Vocabulary

carols: songs
blithe: carefree, happy
hatter: a person who makes hats
noon intermission: lunchtime

Links

"Lift Every Voice and Sing" (10),
"Passing Through Albuquerque" (11)

Springboard

Help students understand the different ways the
various people mentioned in the poem "sing."
Challenge students to update this poem to include
present-day Americans singing: astronaut, teacher,
race car driver, Olympic athlete, and more. Compare
Whitman's view of America in this poem to
Balaban's in "Passing Through Albuquerque" and
Johnson's in "Lift Every Voice and Sing."

Find Out More

about Walt Whitman in
*Teachers and Writers Guide to
Walt Whitman*, Teachers and
Writers Collaborative, 1991,
or in other sources.

4

America the Beautiful (Excerpt)

O beautiful for spacious skies,
For **amber** waves of grain,
For purple mountain **majesties**
Above the fruited plain!
America! America!
God **shed** his grace on thee
And crown thy good with brotherhood
From sea to shining sea!

O beautiful for pilgrim feet
Whose stern **impassioned** stress
A **thoroughfare** of freedom beat
Across the wilderness!
America! America!
God mend thine every **flaw**,
Confirm thy soul in self-control,
Thy liberty in law!

O beautiful for heroes proved
In liberating **strife**.
Who more than self their country loved
And mercy more than life!
America! America!
May God thy gold refine
Till all success be nobleness
And every gain divine!

O beautiful for patriot dream
That sees beyond the years
Thine **alabaster** cities gleam
Undimmed by human tears!
America! America!
God shed his grace on thee
And crown thy good with brotherhood
From sea to shining sea!

—Katherine Lee Bates

Key Vocabulary

amber: golden yellow
majesties: heights of
  power
shed: pour down
impassioned: full of
  passion, enthusiastic
thoroughfare:
  highway, road
flaw: something that
  takes away from or
  spoils completeness
  or perfection
strife: conflict, battle
alabaster: polished
  white stone

Find Out More

about Katherine Lee Bates
and this song in *America
the Beautiful* by Lynn Sherr,
Public Affairs Press, 2001,
or in other sources.

5 America (My Country, 'Tis of Thee) (Excerpt)

My country, 'tis of thee,
sweet land of liberty, of thee I sing;
land where my fathers died,
land of the pilgrims' pride,
from every mountainside let freedom ring!

My native country, thee,
land of the noble free, **thy** name I love;
I love thy rocks and **rills**,
thy woods and templed hills;
my heart with **rapture** thrills, like that above.

Let music swell the breeze,
and ring from all the trees sweet freedom's song;
let **mortal** tongues awake;
let all that breathe **partake**;
let rocks their silence break, the sound prolong . . . .

—Samuel F. Smith

Key Vocabulary

'tis: it is
thee: you
thy: your
rills: streams
rapture: happiness
mortal: human
partake: share, take part in

6 Old man . . .

Old man,
the ancient **tremolo**
rises from your throat
and I know your heart.
In your voice
I hear too
the messages that you saved for me,
from those
you have known.
They are carried
in your voice
like distant thunder.
Allow us to hear
more thunder.
Let it echo
for all time.

—Salli Benedict

Key Vocabulary

tremolo: describes a singer's voice, it is a vibration that adds emotion to the song

Link

"Lincoln Monument: Washington" (9)

Springboard

Ask: What does the poet in this poem want to hear from the "old man"? Compare the last two lines of this poem with the last five lines of "Lincoln Monument: Washington" (9).

7 Red, White, and Blue

Red
is the color of
an apple on a red plate
the red giant
White
is the color of
a white dwarf
Blue
is the color of
the water in a tub
the sky over my head
a cup in the sink
a shirt with a light blue world
on it

my eyes
the ocean
is the smell of
fresh air in the morning

—Devin F. Smith, 5th grader, 2001

Links
"The American Flag" (2),
"Lime Green" (155)

Springboard
Have students write
color poems.

Key Vocabulary

couriers: messengers

Springboard
Ask: "What makes this sentence a
poem? Why is it a good choice to
decorate a post office?"

8 On Their Appointed Rounds

(Inscription on the Main Post Office, New York City)

Neither snow, nor rain,
nor heat, nor gloom of night
stays these **couriers**
from the swift completion
of their appointed rounds.

9 Lincoln Monument: Washington

Let's go see old Abe
Sitting in the marble and the moonlight,
Sitting lonely in the marble and the moonlight,
Quiet for ten thousand centuries, old Abe.
Quiet for a million, million years.

Quiet—

And yet a voice forever
Against the
Timeless walls
Of time—
Old Abe.

—Langston Hughes

Links

"Hymn" (14),
"The New Colossus" (15)

Springboard

Ask: "How can someone be "quiet for ten thousand centuries" and still be a "voice forever"? What did Abraham Lincoln say that could last that long?"

Find Out More

about Langston Hughes in *Langston Hughes: Poet of the Harlem Renaissance* by Christine M. Hill, Enslow, 1997, or in other sources.

 Key Vocabulary

resound: be filled with sound

 **Find Out More**

in a visual representation of the poem in *Lift Every Voice and Sing* by James Weldon Johnson, illustrated by Elizabeth Catlett, Walker, 1993.

10 Lift Every Voice and Sing (Excerpt)

(Also known as the "Negro National Anthem")

Lift every voice and sing
Let it **resound** loud as the rolling sea.
Sing a song full of the faith that the dark past has taught us,
Sing a song full of the hope that the present has brought us.
Facing the rising sun of our new day begun,
Let us march on till victory is won.

—James Weldon Johnson

Passing Through Albuquerque

At dusk, by the irrigation ditch
gurgling past backyards near the highway,
locusts raise a maze of calls in cottonwoods.

A Spanish girl in a white party dress
strolls the **levee** by the muddy water
where her small sister plunks in stones.

Beyond a low **adobe** wall and a wrecked car
men are pitching horseshoes in a dusty lot.
Someone shouts as he clangs in a ringer.

Big winds buffet in ahead of a storm,
rocking the immense trees and whipping up
clouds of dust, wild leaves, and cottonwood.

In the moment when the locusts pause and the girl
presses her up-fluttering dress to her bony knees
you can hear a banjo, guitar, and fiddle

playing "The Mississippi Sawyer" inside a shack.
Moments like that, you can love this country.

—John Balaban

Key Vocabulary

levee: raised river bank
adobe: sun-dried brick

Link

"I Hear America Singing" (3)

Springboard

Discuss the "moment" this poem captures (referred to in the last line).

12

Paul Revere's Ride

Listen, my children, and you shall hear
Of the midnight ride of Paul Revere.
On the eighteenth of April, in Seventy-Five;
Hardly a man is now alive
5   Who remembers that famous day and year.

He said to his friend, "If the British march
By land or sea from the town to-night,
Hang a lantern aloft in the **belfry** arch
Of the North Church tower, as a signal light,—
10   One, if by land, and two, if by sea;
And I on the opposite shore will be,
Ready to ride and spread the alarm
Through every Middlesex village and farm,
For the country-folk to be up and to arm."
15   Then he said "Good-night!" and with muffled oar
Silently rowed to the Charlestown shore,
Just as the moon rose over the bay,
Where swinging wide at her moorings lay
The Somerset, British **man-of-war**;
20   A **phantom** ship, with each mast and **spar**
Across the moon like a prison-bar,
And a huge black hulk, that was magnified
By its own reflection in the tide.

Meanwhile, his friend, through alley and street
25   Wanders and watches with eager ears,
Till in the silence around him he hears
The **muster** of men at the barrack door,
The sound of arms, and the tramp of feet,
And the measured tread of the **grenadiers**,
30   Marching down to their boats on the shore.

Then he climbed the tower of the Old North Church,
By the wooden stairs, with **stealthy** tread,
To the belfry-chamber overhead,
And startled the pigeons from their perch
35   On the **somber** rafters, that round him made
Masses and moving shapes of shade,—
By the trembling ladder, steep and tall,
To the highest window in the wall,
Where he paused to listen and look down
40   A moment on the roofs of the town,
And the moonlight flowing over all.

Beneath, in the churchyard, lay the dead,
In their night-encampment on the hill,
Wrapped in silence so deep and still
45   That he could hear, like a **sentinel**'s tread,
The watchful night-wind, as it went
Creeping along from tent to tent,
And seeming to whisper, "All is well!"
A moment only he feels the spell
50   Of the place and the hour, the secret dread
Of the lonely belfry and the dead;
For suddenly all his thoughts are **bent**
On a shadowy something far away,
Where the river widens to meet the bay,—
55   A line of black, that bends and floats
On the rising tide, like a bridge of boats.

Meanwhile, impatient to mount and ride,
Booted and spurred, with a heavy stride
On the opposite shore walked Paul Revere.
60 Now he patted his horse's side,
Now gazed on the landscape far and near,
Then, **impetuous**, stamped the earth,
And turned and tightened his **saddle-girth**;
But mostly he watched with eager search
65 The belfry-tower of the Old North Church,
As it rose above the graves on the hill,
Lonely and **spectral** and somber and still.
And lo! as he looks, on the belfry's height
A glimmer, and then a gleam of light!
70 He springs to the saddle, the bridle he turns,
But lingers and gazes, till full on his sight
A second lamp in the belfry burns!

A hurry of hoofs in a village street,
A shape in the moonlight, a bulk in the dark,
75 And beneath, from the pebbles, in passing, a spark
Struck out by a **steed** flying fearless and **fleet**:
That was all! And yet, through the gloom and the light,
The fate of a nation was riding that night;
And the spark struck out by that steed, in his flight,
80 Kindled the land into flame with its heat.

He has left the village and mounted the steep,
And beneath him, **tranquil** and broad and deep,
Is the Mystic, meeting the ocean tides;
And under the **alders** that skirt its edge,
85 Now soft on the sand, now loud on the ledge,
Is heard the tramp of his steed as he rides.

It was twelve by the village clock,
When he crossed the bridge into Medford town.
He heard the crowing of the cock,
90 And the barking of the farmer's dog,
And felt the damp of the river fog,
That rises after the sun goes down.

It was one by the village clock,
When he galloped into Lexington.
95 He saw the **gilded weathercock**
Swim in the moonlight as he passed,
And the meeting-house windows, blank and bare,
Gaze at him with a spectral glare,
As if they already stood **aghast**
100 At the bloody work they would look upon.

It was two by the village clock,
When he came to the bridge in Concord town.
He heard the bleating of the flock,
And the twitter of birds among the trees,
105 And felt the breath of the morning breeze
Blowing over the meadows brown.
And one was safe and asleep in his bed
Who at the bridge would be first to fall,
Who that day would be lying dead,
110 Pierced by a British musket-ball.

You know the rest. In the books you have read,
How the **British regulars** fired and fled,—
How the farmers gave them **ball** for ball,
From behind each fence and farm-yard wall,
115   Chasing the red-coats down the lane,
Then crossing the fields to emerge again
Under the trees at the turn of the road,
And only pausing to fire and load.

So through the night rode Paul Revere
120   And so through the night went his cry of alarm
To every Middlesex village and farm,—
A cry of defiance and not of fear,
A voice in the darkness, a knock at the door,
And a word that shall echo forevermore!
125   For, **borne** on the night-wind of the Past,
Through all our history, to the last,
In the hour of darkness and **peril** and need,
The people will waken and listen to hear
The hurrying hoof-beat of that steed,
130   And the midnight-message of Paul Revere.

—Henry Wadsworth Longfellow

Key Vocabulary

belfry: area in a tower where bells hang
man-of-war: ship armed with cannons
phantom: ghostly
spar: wooden pole on a sailing ship
muster: gathering
grenadiers: elite British soldiers
stealthy: moving in a secret manner
somber: sad, gloomy
sentinel: guard
bent: turned
impetuous: impatient
saddle-girth: a strap that holds a saddle on a horse
spectral: ghostly
steed: horse
fleet: very fast
tranquil: peaceful
alders: type of tree
gilded weathercock: golden weathervane
aghast: shocked
British regulars: soldiers
ball: bullet in old-fashioned weapon
borne: carried
peril: danger

Springboard

Read the poem aloud with several students taking a stanza apiece. Discuss the story that's told in the poem. Have students find lines where the author paints vivid pictures (lines 17–25, 59–79, 95–102). Have students write a poem that tells a story from history. Point out that they can start out the same way Longfellow does, "Listen my children and . . ." The poem can rhyme or not, but the story's images should be detailed. Discuss "Hymn," which talks about the events that took place later the same day, thanks to the message carried to Lexington and Concord.

Find Out More

about Paul Revere in *Paul Revere: Boston Patriot* by Augusta Stevenson, Aladdin, 1986, or in other sources. Trace Paul Revere's ride (as described in the poem) on a map of Boston and environs.

Link

Compare "Hymn" (14) with events in this poem, especially lines 110–120.

Barbara Frietchie

13

Up from the meadows rich with corn,
Clear in the cool September morn,

The clustered spires of Frederick stand
Green-walled by the hills of Maryland.

5   Round about them orchards sweep,
Apple and peach trees fruited deep,

Fair as the garden of the Lord
To the eyes of the **famished rebel horde**,

On that pleasant morn of the early fall
10 When **Lee** marched o'er the mountain-wall;

Over the mountains winding down,
Horse and foot, into Frederick town.

Forty flags with their silver stars,
Forty flags with their crimson bars,

15 Flapped in the morning wind: the sun
Of noon looked down, and saw not one.

Up rose old Barbara Frietchie then,
Bowed with her **fourscore** years and ten;

Bravest of all in Frederick town,
20 She took up the flag the men **hauled** down;

In her attic window the **staff** she set,
To show that one heart was loyal yet.

Up the street came the **rebel tread**,
Stonewall Jackson riding ahead.

25 Under his **slouched hat** left and right
He glanced; the old flag met his sight.

"Halt!"—the dust-brown ranks stood fast.
"Fire!"—out blazed the rifle-blast.

It shivered the window, pane and sash;
30 It rent the banner with seam and gash.

Quick, as it fell, from the broken staff
Dame Barbara snatched the **silken scarf**.

She leaned far out on the window-sill,
And shook it forth with a royal will.

35 "Shoot, if you must, this old gray head,
But spare your country's flag," she said.

A shade of sadness, a blush of shame,
Over the face of the leader came;

The nobler nature within him stirred
40 To life at that woman's deed and word;

"Who touches a hair of **yon** gray head
Dies like a dog! March on!" he said.

All day long through Frederick street
Sounded the tread of marching feet:

45 All day long that free flag **tost**
Over the heads of the rebel **host**.

Ever its torn folds rose and fell
On the loyal winds that loved it well;

And through the hill gaps sunset light
50 Shone over it with a warm good-night.

Barbara Frietchie's work is o'er,
And the Rebel rides on his raids no more.

Honor to her! and let a tear
Fall, for her sake, on Stonewall's **bier**.

55 Over Barbara Frietchie's grave,
Flag of Freedom and Union, wave!

Peace and order and beauty draw
Round **thy** symbol of light and law;

And ever the stars above look down
60 On **thy stars** below in Frederick town!

—John Greenleaf Whittier

Key Vocabulary

famished rebel horde:
large group of starving
Confederate soldiers
Lee: Confederate General
Robert E. Lee
fourscore: 80 (four times
20, a "score")
hauled: pulled
staff: stick the flag hangs
from
rebel tread: footsteps of
Rebel (Confederate)
soldiers

Stonewall Jackson:
Confederate General
slouched hat: soft hat
with wide brim
Dame: honorary title
silken scarf: the flag
yon: the one over there
tost: tossed
host: crowd
bier: coffin
thy: your
thy stars: the flag

14

Hymn

Sung at the Dedication of the Concord Monument, April 19, 1836

By the **rude** bridge that arched the flood,
Their flag to April's breeze unfurled,
Here once the embattled farmers stood
And fired the shot heard round the world.
The foe long since in silence slept;
Alike the conqueror silent sleeps;
And Time the ruined bridge has swept
Down the dark stream that seaward creeps.
On this green bank, by this soft stream,
We set today a **votive** stone;
That memory may their deed redeem,
When, like our **sires**, our sons are gone.
Spirit, that made those heroes dare
To die, and leave their children free,
Bid Time and Nature gently spare
The **shaft** we raise to them and thee.

—Ralph Waldo Emerson

Key Vocabulary

rude: rough
votive: in honor of
sires: ancestors
shaft: monument

15 The New Colossus

Not like the **brazen giant of Greek fame**
With conquering limbs **astride** from land to land;
Here at our sea-washed, sunset gates shall stand
A mighty woman with a torch, whose flame
Is the imprisoned lightning, and her name
Mother of Exiles. From her beacon-hand
Glows world-wide welcome; her mild eyes command
The air-bridged harbor that twin cities frame,
"Keep, ancient lands, your **storied pomp**!" cries she
With silent lips. "Give me your tired, your poor,
Your huddled masses yearning to breathe free,
The wretched **refuse** of your **teeming** shore,
Send these, the homeless, **tempest-tossed** to me,
I lift my lamp beside the golden door!"

—Emma Lazarus

Key Vocabulary

brazen giant of Greek fame: the Colossus of Rhodes, a huge bronze statue of the Greek god Apollo
astride: one leg on either side
storied pomp: historic ceremonies
refuse: seen as worthless
teeming: crowded
tempest-tossed: shaken up by storms

 **Link**

"The Statue of Liberty" (16)

16 The Statue of Liberty

I stand in New York Harbor,
  very proud and tall
in my hand I hold a torch,
  to light the way for all.
I welcome everyone who comes,
  whether short or tall,
I am there to greet the people,
  Freedom for all!

—Lauren Strainge,
5th grader, 2001

 **Find Out More**

about the Statue of Liberty in *The Statue of Liberty* by Debra Hess, Benchmark Books, 2003, or in other sources. Investigate children's contributions to the building of the Statue of Liberty.

 **Link** "The New Colossus" (15)

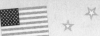

17 · We Are a Living People

Read at Wisconsin Senate Education Committee hearing on March 15, 2000

I don't understand. . . .
Why should anyone's identity be defined by your games?
We are a living people.
Why are we used as entertainment for schools?
We are a living people.
Why must we be used as nicknames, logos, and mascots?
We are a living people.
Why must we, a living people, be singled out?
Why must we, a living people, be stereotyped?
Can't you tell who we, a living people, are?
Why doesn't what we say matter?
We are a living people.
Why don't our voices count?
We are a living people.
How can you say "All Men are Created Equal . . ."
But not *create [teams with names like] the Mishicot Caucasians
or the Gale-Ettrick Blackmen?*
Why do you treat us, a living people, as relics?
Why is our culture for sale?
We are a living people.
Why must we fight, for that given to others?
We are a living people.
I don't understand. . . . .
Respect should be such a simple thing?
Respect should be such a simple thing!
Why do you make it so hard?
Why do we make it so hard?

—Lori Wautier

Springboard

Ask: "Who does the poet mean by 'a living people'? What stereotypes is the poet trying to correct? What are the 'nicknames, logos, and mascots' she refers to in line 6?" Read aloud, alternating voices.

Find Out More

about native people's objections to team names and logos such as the Atlanta Braves and Washington Redskins.

18

Oriflamme

"I can remember when I was a little, young girl, how my old mammy would sit out of doors in the evenings and look up at the stars and groan, and I would say, 'Mammy, what makes you groan so?' And she would say, 'I am groaning to think of my poor children; they do not know where I be and I don't know where they be. I look up at the stars and they look up at the stars!'"

— Sojourner Truth

I think I see her sitting bowed and black,
Stricken and **seared** with slavery's mortal scars,
'Reft of her children, lonely, anguished, yet
Still looking at the stars.

Symbolic mother, we thy **myriad** sons,
Pounding our stubborn hearts on **Freedom's bars**,
Clutching our birthright, fight with faces set,
Still visioning the stars!

— Jessie Fauset

Key Vocabulary

oriflamme: an inspiring symbol that energizes people involved in a struggle

seared: burned

[be]reft of: without, deprived of

myriad: many

Freedom's bars: the laws and practices keeping African Americans from full freedom

Link

"Lift Every Voice and Sing" (10)

Springboard

Discuss why looking up at the stars is such a powerful symbol of desire for freedom and equality.

Find Out More

about Sojourner Truth in *Sojourner Truth* (In Their Own Words series) by Peter Roop, Scholastic, 2003, or in other sources. Identify other "oriflammes" (inspiring symbols) in American history and in the civil rights struggle.

19 Frederick Douglass

When it is finally ours, this freedom, this liberty, this beautiful
and terrible thing, needful to man as air,
usable as earth; when it belongs at last to all,
when it is truly instinct, brain matter, **diastole**, **systole**,
reflex action; when it is finally won; when it is more
than the gaudy mumbo jumbo of politicians:
this man, this Douglass, this former slave, this Negro
beaten to his knees, exiled, visioning a world
where none is lonely, none hunted, alien,
this man, superb in love and logic, this man
shall be remembered. Oh, not with statues' **rhetoric**,
not with legends and poems and wreaths of bronze alone,
but with the lives grown out of his life, the lives
fleshing his dream of the beautiful, needful thing.

—Robert Hayden

 Key Vocabulary

diastole and **systole:** the two parts of a heart beat
rhetoric: a formal way of speaking

Link

"Oriflamme" (18)

 **Springboard**

Ask: "Where does the first sentence of this poem end? How does the poet want Frederick Douglass to be remembered?"

 **Find Out More**

about Frederick Douglass in *Frederick Douglass* (History Makers series) by Catherine Welch, Lerner Publishing Group, 2003, or in other sources.

The Women Who Went to the Field

20

Key Vocabulary

betwixt: between

chanced: happened

clammy: sweaty and cold

parched: thirsty

delirium's strife: struggle with a high fever

quail: pull back fearfully

unsanctioned: not allowed

oft times: often

the lines: battle lines where soldiers fought the Civil War

implored: begged

consolers: people who comfort others

Springboard

According to the poem, what were women supposed to do in wartime? How does Clara Barton describe the contribution of women who went to war? How does she explain why women like herself left home to be on the front line during the Civil War?

Find Out More

about Clara Barton in *Clara Barton: Founder of the Red Cross* by Augusta Stevenson, Aladdin, 1986, or in other sources.

The women who went to the field, you say, . . .
What did they go for? Just to be in the way!—
They'd not know the difference **betwixt** work and play,
What did they know about war anyway?
5 What could they do? of what use could they be?
They would scream at the sight of a gun, don't you see? . . .
And thus it was settled by common consent, . . .
[By] husbands, or brothers, or whoever went,
That the place for the women was in their own homes,
10 There to patiently wait until victory comes.
But later, it **chanced**, just how no one knew,
That the lines slipped a bit, and some [be]gan to crowd through;
And they went, where did they go? Ah; where did they not?
Show us the battle, the field, or the spot
15 Where the groans of the wounded rang out on the air
That her ear caught it not, and her hand was not there,
Who wiped the death sweat from the cold **clammy** brow,
And sent home the message;—"'Tis well with him Now"?
Who watched in the tents, whilst the fever fires burned,
20 And the pain-tossing limbs in agony turned,
And wet the **parched** tongue, calmed **delirium's strife**
Till the dying lips murmured, "My Mother," "My Wife"! . . . .
Did these women **quail** at the sight of a gun?
Will some soldier tell us of one he saw run? . . . .
25 [T]hese were the women who went to the war:
The women of question; what did they go for? . . .
They saw, in high purpose, a duty to do,
And the armor of right broke the barriers through.
Uninvited, unaided, **unsanctioned oft times**,
30 With pass, or without it, they pressed on **the lines**;
They pressed, they **implored**, till they ran the lines through,
And this was the "running" the men saw them do. . . .
And what would they do if war came again? . . .
They would stand with you now, as they stood with you then,
35 The nurses, **consolers**, and saviors of men.

—Clara Barton

21 Adowe

When the center fire burns high
      you will thank
      the earth for this home
              the waters
              corn and the fruit
              the medicines
              the trees
for their usefulness
              the animals
for their flesh and furs
              birds
for songs and beautiful feathers
you will thank
              the winds
              the thunder
              the sun
              and grandmother moon
you will thank
              the women
              hunter
              warrior
              children
you will thank
              the hand
which has placed
these creatures about you
and which is the source
of health and life
I
am thankful

—Maurice Kenny

Key Vocabulary

adowe: thanks

22 · April Rain Song

Let the rain kiss you
Let the rain beat upon your head with silver liquid drops
Let the rain sing you a lullaby
The rain makes still pools on the sidewalk
The rain makes running pools in the gutter
The rain plays a little sleep song on our roof at night
And I love the rain.

—Langston Hughes

23 · Watching Wolves

Will walks out in the snowy field,
He's looking for wolves to watch.
His boots crunch on the snow.
On the far side of the field,
Behind the fringe of firs
Wolves watch Will.

—Susan Moger

24 · Winter Poem

once a snowflake fell
on my brow and i loved
it so much and i kissed
it and it was happy and called its cousins
and brothers and a web
of snow engulfed me then
i reached to love them all
and i squeezed them and they became
a spring rain and i stood perfectly
still and was a flower

—Nikki Giovanni

Find Out More

about the poet and read more of her poems in *Nikki Giovanni: Poet of the People* by Judith Pinkerton Josephson, Enslow, 2000, or in other sources.

25 The Little Turtle

There was a little turtle.
He lived in a box.
He swam in a puddle.
He climbed on the rocks.
He snapped at a mosquito,
He snapped at a flea.
He snapped at a **minnow**.
And he snapped at me.
He caught the mosquito.
He caught the flea.
He caught the minnow.
But he didn't catch me.

—Vachel Lindsay

Key Vocabulary

minnow: very small fish

Springboard

Ask students to identify the repeated words, *he snapped at* and *he caught* and discuss how the repetition builds expectations and adds punch to the surprise ending. Three students can read this poem, one to read the first four lines, one to read the "He snapped" section, and one to read the "He caught" section.

26 The Cow

The friendly cow all red and white,
I love with all my heart:
She gives me cream with all her might,
To eat with apple-tart.

She wanders lowing here and there,
And yet she cannot stray,
All in the pleasant open air,
The pleasant light of day.

And blown by all the winds that pass
And wet with all the showers,
She walks among the meadow grass
And eats the meadow flowers.

—Robert Louis Stevenson

Links

Other poems from
A Child's Garden of Verses (158–161)

27

Look at Six Eggs

Look at six eggs
In a mockingbird's nest.

Listen to six mockingbirds
Flinging follies of **O-be-joyful**
Over the marshes and uplands.

Look at songs
Hidden in eggs.

—Carl Sandburg

Key Vocabulary

flinging: throwing
follies: silliness
O-be-joyful: the mockingbird's song

28

A White Hen Sitting

A white hen sitting
On white eggs three:
Next, three **speckled** chickens
As plump as plump can be.
An owl, and a hawk,
And a bat come to see:
But chicks beneath their mother's wing
Squat safe as safe can be.

—Christina Rossetti

Key Vocabulary

speckled: covered with small spots

29

Give Me the Splendid, Silent Sun (Excerpt)

Give me the splendid silent sun, with all his beams full-dazzling;
Give me juicy autumnal fruit, ripe and red from the orchard;
Give me a field where the unmow'd grass grows;
Give me an arbor, give me the **trellis'd** grape;
Give me fresh corn and wheat—give me serene-moving animals, teaching content;
Give me nights perfectly quiet, as on high plateaus west of the Mississippi, and I looking up at the stars;
Give me **odorous** at sunrise a garden of beautiful flowers, where I can walk undisturb'd. . . .

—Walt Whitman

Key Vocabulary

trellis'd: a fence for holding up plants
odorous: fragrant

Link

"I Hear America Singing" (3)

30

Bare Feet and Dog

Lovey, my chocolate Lab,
Swims in the creek
Shakes water on my feet
Thumps her tail on my feet
Steps on my feet
Tangles up her leash in my feet
Slurps water from her bowl then
Licks my feet.

She has beautiful eyes and a loud bark
She's afraid of thunder but not the dark
Lovey is there for me and always sweet
I love her from my head down to my
sore, wet feet.

—Susan Moger

31

Panda Dreams

For the pandas at the National Zoo

Pandas, I see you in there.
Won't you please come out?
I came to the zoo to ask you,
"What do you dream about?"
Do you dream you're home in China?
Do you dream you're on a bus?
Do you dream that you're outside the fence—
Looking in at us?

—Susan Moger

32 The Eagle

He clasps the **crag** with crooked hands;
Close to the sun in lonely lands,
Ring'd with the **azure** world, he stands.

The wrinkled sea beneath him crawls;
He watches from his mountain walls,
And like a thunderbolt he falls.

—Alfred, Lord Tennyson

Key Vocabulary

crag: cliff
azure: sky-blue

Springboard

Ask: "What action takes place in this poem? What strengths of the eagle does the poet describe? What words convey how high the eagle is above the sea?" The poem is a *tercet*, composed of 3-line stanzas. Have students write a tercet with the same rhyme pattern (aaa, bbb).

Key Vocabulary

substantially transparent: light passes through them
ethereal: delicate, not part of the real world

Springboard

Have students find all the verbs that the poet uses to describe the actions of the fireflies.

33 Fireflies

fireflies on night canvas
cat eyes glowing like moonbeams
climbing now towards hidden places
they speak to the language
of darkness & of their lives torn
from roots in flux & of their substance
forming the core
substantially transparent they
swim through **ethereal** darkness
where silence can be wisdom
searching for open doors

—Quincy Troupe

34 Insects

Insects
Buzzing, flying
Crawling, stinging, biting
Caterpillars, butterflies, moths
Scary

—Sam DiTonno, 5th Grader, 2002

Link

"Brother in Hospital" (88),
"The American Flag" (2)

Springboard

Have students try writing cinquains
(see page 14).

35 The Butterfly

I am a shy little butterfly
When you get close, me oh my!

I'm never sure whether to stay or flee
What would keep you from noticing me?

Life was easier when I lived on the ground,
Crawling slowly all around.

All I did was eat and eat
Until the day I tired my feet.

I made a home in the tree below,
Hanging and rocking to and fro.

When time was up, I poked a hole
And out I came, a beautiful soul.

So, lay still upon the grass
Watch me flutter, watch me pass.

—Cathy Bamji

Links

"Fireflies" (33),
"White Butterflies" (36)

Springboard

Have students read aloud and
use hand gestures to portray the
progression of the butterfly's life
revealed in the poem. Compare
this poet's vision of butterflies
with Quincy Troupe's "Fireflies."
Ask students to describe the
experience of reading the two
poems. Which poem requires
more attention? Which poem do
they prefer and why?

36 White Butterflies

Fly, white butterflies, out to sea,
Frail pale wings for the winds to try,
Small white wings that we scarce can see
Fly.

Here and there may a chance-caught eye
Note in a **score** of you **twain** or three
Brighter or darker of **tinge** or dye.

Some fly light as a laugh of **glee**,
Some fly soft as a low long sigh:
All to the **haven** where each would be
Fly.

—Algernon Charles Swinburne

Key Vocabulary

frail: fragile, delicate
score: twenty
twain: two
tinge: a faint touch of color
glee: happiness
haven: safe place

Links

"Fireflies" (33),
"The Butterfly" (35)

Springboard

Ask: "What words does the poet use to distinguish butterflies from each other? What does the poet want the butterflies to do?" Compare this poem to "The Butterfly" and "Fireflies." Ask: "In your opinion, which of the three poets best describes his or her subject?"

37 Squirrel Hill

Roses and peonies and daffy-down-dillies
Apple trees, peach trees, and lovely white lilies
Blueberries, strawberries, and wild cherries too,
Dogwood and laurel and wild onions—phew!
All this in springtime on Squirrel Hill—
Sometimes I wish we lived there still.

—Susan Moger

38 Tiger

T reacherous, sharp claws
I nvincible, yellow teeth
G igantic, furry paws
E normously strong jaws
R estless and beautiful

—Andi Overbaugh, 5th grader, 2002

Links

"Whales" (40), "Nubian Goats" (43), "Sledding" (51)

Springboard

After reading this and other name poems, have students write name poems of their own about topics in science and social studies.

39 Schools of Whales

Schools of whales have art
And gym and music
Little whales are very smart
And don't get seasick.

—Susan Moger

40 Whales

W hen they jump out of the water
   they soar higher than the sun
H ow beautiful they are
   when they swim,
A s they splash with their enormous fins.
L oving and caring for their young
E arly in the morning you can hear them sing
S uch magnificent creatures.

—Tasheena Stevens, 5th grader, 2003

Last Leaf

41

Long look down
Fall to ground
Happy to be
      Red or orange
           Or even brown
                Happy to be
                    Falling down
Look left, look right
Twirl around after night
    Sunlight's bright
    It's all right
To be last leaf on the tree—
    Just shout: "look at me!"
    And let go
    ". . . Oh
    . . . . Oh
    . . . . . Oh
    . . . . . Oh
        Gee
        Whiz
        Golly
        Gosh!"
Last leaf down
To the ground!

—Shirley Johannesen Levine

Springboard

Have students write a poem about being the "last" something: the last flower, the last stop on the school bus, the last doughnut on the plate.

42 The Birthright

We who were born
In country places,
Far from cities
And shifting faces,
We have a **birthright**
No man can sell,
And a secret joy
No man can tell.

For we are **kindred**
To lordly things,
The wild duck's flight
And the white owl's wings;
To pike and salmon,
To bull and horse,
The **curlew**'s cry
And the smell of **gorse**.

Pride of trees,
Swiftness of streams,
Magic of frost
Have shaped our dreams:
No baser vision
Their spirit fills
Who walk by right
On the naked hills.

—Eiluned Lewis

Key Vocabulary

birthright: a right that a person is entitled to by birth
kindred: in the same family, related to
curlew: a long-legged shore bird
gorse: thick shrub with yellow flowers

43 Nubian Goats

N ibble on your shoes
U tterly playful
B ig floppy ears
I ndependent
A dorable
N ation's #1 goat

G ood to cuddle with
O ats are bad for them
A good family project animal
T errible, picky eaters
S tubborn

—Samantha Lundstrom,
5th grader, 2003

Birches

44

When I see birches bend to left and right
Across the lines of straighter darker trees,
I like to think some boy's been swinging them.
But swinging doesn't bend them down to stay.
5   Ice-storms do that. Often you must have seen them

Loaded with ice a sunny winter morning
After a rain. They click upon themselves
As the breeze rises, and turn many-colored
As the stir cracks and crazes their enamel.
10   Soon the sun's warmth makes them shed crystal shells

Shattering and avalanching on the snow-crust—
Such heaps of broken glass to sweep away
You'd think the inner dome of heaven had fallen.
They are dragged to the withered **bracken** by the load,
15   And they seem not to break; though once they are bowed

So low for long, they never right themselves:
You may see their trunks arching in the woods
Years afterwards, trailing their leaves on the ground
Like girls on hands and knees that throw their hair
20   Before them over their heads to dry in the sun.

But I was going to say when Truth broke in
With all her matter-of-fact about the ice-storm
(Now am I free to be poetical?)
I should prefer to have some boy bend them
25   As he went out and in to fetch the cows—

Some boy too far from town to learn baseball,
Whose only play was what he found himself,
Summer or winter, and could play alone.
One by one he subdued his father's trees
30   By riding them down over and over again

Until he took the stiffness out of them,
And not one but hung limp, not one was left
For him to conquer. He learned all there was
To learn about not launching out too soon
35 And so not carrying the tree away

Clear to the ground. He always kept his poise
To the top branches, climbing carefully
With the same pains you use to fill a cup
Up to the brim, and even above the brim.
40 Then he flung outward, feet first, with a swish,

Kicking his way down through the air to the ground.
So was I once myself a swinger of birches.
And so I dream of going back to be.
It's when I'm weary of considerations,
45 And life is too much like a pathless wood

Where your face burns and tickles with the cobwebs
Broken across it, and one eye is weeping
From a twig's having lashed across it open.
I'd like to get away from earth awhile
50 And then come back to it and begin over.

May no fate willfully misunderstand me
And half grant what I wish and snatch me away
Not to return. Earth's the right place for love:
I don't know where it's likely to go better.
55 I'd like to go by climbing a birch tree,

And climb black branches up a snow-white trunk
Toward heaven, till the tree could bear no more,
But dipped its top and set me down again.
That would be good both going and coming back.
60 One could do worse than be a swinger of birches.

—Robert Frost

Key Vocabulary

bracken: a large fern

 Springboard

Help students identify and understand the parts of the poem that tell precisely how to swing on a birch tree. Invite them to write poems about an activity they enjoy, including details about what they like to do and ending their poems the way Frost does: "One could do worse than be a . . . (a walker of dogs, a player of computer games, a rider of dirt bikes)."

Find Out More

about Robert Frost in *Robert Frost* (Bloom's Major Poets) by Harold Bloom, Chelsea House Publications, 1998, or in other sources.

45

Chamber Music XXXV

　　All day I hear the noise of waters
Making moan,
　　Sad as the sea-bird is when, going
Forth alone,
　　He hears the winds cry to the water's
Monotone.
　　The grey winds, the cold winds are blowing
Where I go.
　　I hear the noise of many waters
Far below.
　　All day, all night, I hear them flowing
To and fro.

—James Joyce

Key Vocabulary

monotone: steady one-note sound that doesn't change
to and fro: back and forth

Link

"Sea Slant" (110)

Key Vocabulary

unhasting: unhurried, slow
larboard: left side of boat, port side

46

On the Mississippi

Through wild and tangled forests
　　The broad, **unhasting** river flows—
　　Spotted with rain-drops, gray with night;
Upon its curving breast there goes
　　A lonely steamboat's **larboard** light,
A blood-red star against the shadowy oaks;
　　Noiseless as a ghost, through greenish gleam
　　Of fire-flies, before the boat's wild scream—
A heron flaps away
Like silence taking flight.

—Hamlin Garland

47 The Cataract at Lodore (Excerpt)

The **cataract** strong
Then plunges along,
Striking and raging
As if a war raging
5 Its caverns and rocks among;
Rising and leaping,
Sinking and creeping,
Swelling and sweeping,
Showering and springing,
10 Flying and flinging,
Writhing and ringing,
Eddying and whisking,
Spouting and frisking,
Turning and twisting,
15 Around and around
With endless rebound . . .

And darting and parting,
And threading and spreading,
And whizzing and hissing,
20 And dripping and skipping,
And hitting and splitting,
And shining and twining,
And rattling and battling,
And shaking and quaking,
25 And pouring and roaring,
And waving and raving,
And tossing and crossing,
And flowing and going,
And running and stunning,
30 And foaming and roaming,
And dinning and spinning,
And dropping and hopping,
And working and jerking,
And guggling and struggling,
35 And heaving and **cleaving**,
And moaning and groaning;

And glittering and **frittering**,
And gathering and feathering,
And whitening and brightening,
40 And quivering and shivering,
And hurrying and **skurrying**,
And thundering and **floundering**;

Dividing and gliding and sliding,
And falling and brawling and sprawling,
45 And driving and **riving** and striving,
And sprinkling and twinkling and wrinkling,
And sounding and bounding and rounding,
And bubbling and troubling and doubling,
And grumbling and rumbling and tumbling,
50 And clattering and battering and shattering;

Retreating and beating and meeting and sheeting,
Delaying and straying and playing and spraying,
Advancing and prancing and glancing and dancing,
Recoiling, turmoiling and toiling and boiling,
55 And gleaming and streaming and steaming and beaming,
And rushing and flushing and brushing and gushing,
And flapping and rapping and clapping and slapping,
And curling and whirling and **purling** and twirling,
And thumping and plumping and bumping and jumping,
60 And dashing and flashing and splashing and clashing; . . .
All at once and all **o'er**, with a mighty uproar,—
And this way the water comes down at Lodore.

—Robert Southey

Key Vocabulary

cataract: a large waterfall, a rush of water
cleaving: holding on to
frittering: wasting time
skurrying (scurrying): hurrying along
floundering: moving with stumbling or plunging motions
riving: breaking into pieces
purling: flowing and making a soft sound
o'er: over

Link

"The Bells" (149)

Springboard

Challenge students to list adjectives and nouns used in the poem to describe the power of water. Use a thesaurus to add more words about water's power. Compare the rhythm and power of language in this poem with "The Bells" (149).

The Wild Swans at Coole

48

The trees are in their autumn beauty,
The woodland paths are dry,
Under the October twilight the water
Mirrors a still sky;
5 Upon the brimming water among the stones
Are nine and fifty swans.

The nineteenth Autumn has come upon me
Since I first made my count;
I saw, before I had well finished,
10 All suddenly mount
And scatter wheeling in great broken rings
Upon their **clamorous** wings.

I have looked upon those brilliant creatures,
And now my heart is sore.
15 All's changed since I, hearing at twilight,
The first time on this shore,
The bell-beat of their wings above my head,
Trod with a lighter tread.

Unwearied still, lover by lover,
20 They paddle in the cold,
Companionable streams or climb the air;
Their hearts have not grown old;
Passion or conquest, wander where they will,
Attend upon them still.

25 But now they drift on the still water
Mysterious, beautiful;
Among what rushes will they build,
By what lake's edge or pool
Delight men's eyes, when I awake some day
30 To find they have flown away?

—William Butler Yeats

Key Vocabulary

clamorous: noisy
trod: walked

Link

"Improved Farm Land" (49), "The Song of Wandering Aengus" (147)

Springboard

Compare this poem to Yeats's "The Song of Wandering Aengus." How are the two poems alike? How are they different?

49 Improved Farm Land

Tall timber stood here once, here on a corn belt farm along the **Monon**.

Here the roots of a half-mile of trees dug their **runners** deep in the **loam** for a grip and a hold against wind storms.

Then the axemen came and the chips flew to the zing of steel and handle—
the **lank railsplitters** cut the big ones first, the beeches and the oaks, then the brush.

Dynamite, wagons, and horses took the stumps—the plows sunk their teeth in—
now it is first class corn land—improved property—and the hogs grunt
over the **fodder crops**.

It would come hard now for this half mile of improved farm land along the Monon corn belt, on a piece of Grand Prairie, to remember once it had a great singing family of trees.

—Carl Sandburg

Key Vocabulary

Monon: a creek in northwestern central Indiana

runners: roots

loam: loose dirt

lank: tall and thin

railsplitters: men who cut wood for fences

fodder crops: food for animals

Link

"The Wild Swans at Coole" (48)

Springboard

Explain how Yeats's "The Wild Swans at Coole" (48) foretells a future loss of natural beauty, while in "Improved Farm Land" Sandburg is already mourning the "great singing family of trees." Read some of the other Sandburg poems in this collection ("Fog" (52) and "Primer Lesson" (131)) and talk about his images and word choices. How are they different? Investigate what animals and trees are native to your locality or state. What trees were cut down to build your town?

Find Out More

Read more poems by Carl Sandburg in *The Complete Poems of Carl Sandburg*, Harcourt, 2003.

50

How One Winter Came in the Lake Region

 Key Vocabulary

blear: dimmed or blurred
gnarlèd: twisted
runnels: banks of streams
aghast: shocked
sere: withered, dry
tremor: shaking
strains: music
withered: shrunken, dried up

For weeks and weeks the autumn world stood still,
    Clothed in the shadow of a smoky haze;
The fields were dead, the wind had lost its will,
And all the lands were hushed by wood and hill,
5   In those grey, withered days.
Behind a mist the **blear** sun rose and set,
    At night the moon would nestle in a cloud;
The fisherman, a ghost, did cast his net;
The lake its shores forgot to chafe and fret,
10   And hushed its caverns loud.
Far in the smoky woods the birds were mute,
    Save that from blackened tree a jay would scream,
Or far in swamps the lizard's lonesome lute
Would pipe in thirst, or by some **gnarlèd** root
15   The tree-toad trilled his dream.
From day to day still hushed by season's mood,
    The streams stayed in their **runnels** shrunk and dry;
Suns rose **aghast** by wave and shore and wood,
And all the world, with ominous silence, stood
20   In weird expectancy:
When one strange night the sun like blood went down,
    Flooding the heavens in a ruddy hue;
Red grew the lake, the **sere** fields parched and brown,
Red grew the marshes where the creeks stole down,
25   But never a wind-breath blew.
That night I felt the winter in my veins,
    A joyous **tremor** of the icy glow;
And woke to hear the north's wild vibrant **strains**,
While far and wide, by **withered** woods and plains,
30 Fast fell the driving snow.

—Wilfred Campbell

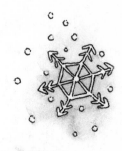

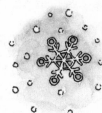

51 | Sledding

S peeding down a hill,
L ow on my sled,
E ating the flakes that fly in my mouth,
D igging my gloves in the snow,
D riving myself through trees,
 I n and out in and out,
N ow up a high jump,
G ripping my sled.

—Spencer Bassette, 5th grader, 2001

52 | Fog

The fog comes
on little cat feet.
It sits looking
over harbor and city
on silent haunches
and then moves on.

—Carl Sandburg

Links

Haiku (66–75)

Springboard

Explain that this type of poetry is called free verse. In being unrhymed it is similar to haiku (see Introduction, page 13). Explain that Sandburg, who had read haiku, was probably influenced by it in writing this poem. Ask: "What is Sandburg comparing the fog to? How do you know?"

53 | Who Has Seen the Wind?

Who has seen the wind?
Neither I nor you:
But when the leaves hang trembling
The wind is passing through.
Who has seen the wind?
Neither you nor I:
But when the trees bow down their heads
The wind is passing by.

—Christina Rossetti

54 | The Wind

The wind an amazing
Power doth **wield**;
He can shape **snow-maidens**
And send them dancing **o'er** the field.

He, with gentle breath,
In the warmth of spring,
Can coax the little birds
To take to the wing.

He, in a drought,
The rain clouds can blow,
Till the parched ground is drenched
And the river churning flows.

He the leaves **doth** take
From their perches,
When autumn demands offering
Of maples, oaks, and birches.

The wind an amazing
Power doth command;
He can shape snow-maidens
And send them dancing o'er the land.

—Rachel Moger-Reischer

Key Vocabulary

wield: command, use
snow-maidens: shapes formed by snow blowing in the wind
o'er: over
doth: does

55 The Storm

See lightning is flashing,
The forest is crashing,
The rain will come dashing,
 A flood will be rising **anon**;

The heavens are scowling,
The thunder is growling,
The loud winds are howling,
 The storm has come suddenly on!

But now the sky clears,
The bright sun appears,
Now nobody fears,
 But soon every cloud will be gone.

—Sara Coleridge

Key Vocabulary

anon: soon

Key Vocabulary

vale: valley
frail: fragile, delicate

Link

"I Wandered Lonely as a Cloud" (148)

Springboard

Compare descriptions of daffodils in this poem and in Wordsworth's "I Wandered Lonely as a Cloud."

56 Daffadowndilly

Growing in the **vale**
By the uplands hilly,
Growing straight and **frail**,
Lady Daffadowndilly.
In a golden crown,
And a scant green gown
While the spring blows chilly,
Lady Daffadown,
Sweet Daffadowndilly

—Christina Rossetti

57 Wrens and Robins in the Hedge

Wrens and robins in the hedge,
Wrens and robins here and there;
Building, perching, pecking, fluttering,
Everywhere!

—Christina Rossetti

58 On the Grassy Banks

On the grassy banks
Lambkins at their pranks;
Woolly sisters, woolly brothers
Jumping off their feet
While their woolly mothers
Watch by them and bleat.

—Christina Rossetti

Key Vocabulary

lambkins: lambs

59 April

The roofs are shining from the rain.
The sparrows twitter as they fly,
And with a windy April grace
The little clouds go by.
Yet the back-yards are bare and brown
With only one unchanging tree—
I could not be so sure of Spring
Save that it sings in me.

—Sara Teasdale

60 | Song (Excerpt)

Oh! To be a flower
Nodding in the sun,
Bending, then upspringing
As the breezes run;
Holding up
A scent-brimmed cup,
Full of summer's fragrance to the
summer sun.

—Amy Lowell

61 | When I Heard the Learned Astronomer

When I heard the **learned** astronomer,
When the proofs, the figures, were ranged in columns before me,
When I was shown the charts and diagrams, to add, divide and measure them,
When I sitting heard the astronomer where he lectured with much applause in the lecture-room,
How soon **unaccountable** I became tired and sick,
How soon rising and gliding out I wandered off by myself,
In the mystical moist night-air, and from time to time,
Looked up in perfect silence at the stars.

—Walt Whitman

Key Vocabulary

learned: well-educated
unaccountable: for no apparent reason

Ask: "Is Whitman saying we don't need astronomers? How does the repetition of 'When I . . .' add to the mood of the poem?"

Find Out More

about the poet in *Walt Whitman: Words for America* by Barbara Kerley, Scholastic Press, 2004, or in other sources.

62 Milk-White Moon, Put the Cows to Sleep

Milk-white moon, put the cows to sleep
Since five o'clock in the morning,
Since they stood up out of the grass,
Where they have slept on their knees and **hocks**,
They have eaten grass and given their milk,
And kept their heads and teeth at the earth's face.
Now they are looking at you, milk-white moon.
Carelessly as they look at the level landscapes,
Carelessly as they look at a pail of new white milk,
They are looking at you, wondering not at all, at all.
If the moon is the skim face top of a pail of milk
Wondering not at all, carelessly looking.
Put the cows to sleep, milk-white moon,
Put the cows to sleep.

—Carl Sandburg

Key Vocabulary

hocks: joint in the back legs of four-legged animals (similar to knees in front legs)

63 The Horses of the Sea

The horses of the sea
Rear a foaming **crest**,
But the horses of the land
Serve us the best.
The horses of the land
Munch corn and clover,
While the foaming sea-horses
Toss and turn over.

—Christina Rossetti

Key Vocabulary

rear: rise up
crest: top of a wave

Links

"Scents of the Ocean" (64),
"I Walked to the Beach" (65)

Springboard

Use this poem to inspire students to write a poem using a metaphor (like horses/waves) about a feature of the natural world.

64 Scents of the Ocean

The salt smell of the ocean
That smells so good
   all the way from town
The wind and waves blow your
   hair,
The salty sand swoops from
   the air,
The sun beating down,
The windy smell that blows
   to my nose,
The fishy smell that winds
   through the air,
The salt smell of the ocean.

—Christina Baker, 5th grader, 2002

65 I Walked to the Beach

I walked to the beach,
I looked up into the sky
and saw the sun with her golden hair.

She smiles at me with her beautiful
shining teeth.
All I can do is grin.

As I'm swimming in the ocean she
makes sure that she is as bright as ever.

As I lie down on my towel,
she keeps me toasty warm.

The day is over and she kisses me
goodbye on the cheek
with her burning lips.

—Samantha Seney, 5th grader, 2002

Links

"The Horses of the Sea" (63),
"Scents of the Ocean" (64)

Springboard

Use this poem and "Scents of the Ocean" (64) to inspire students to write their own "sense" poems about a place, drawing on sight, scent, touch, taste, and hearing.

Haiku

66

Spring grass is peaceful
Wind rustles in the deep green blades
All is quiet now.

—Caitlin Peterson, 4th grader, 2000

Springboard

Introduce the class to haiku and senryu, or review what you have already studied (see Introduction, page 13). Then read the following poems. Note that some are translated from the Japanese and that the syllable count of the translated words doesn't always fit the prescribed number. Encourage students to write haiku (seasonal or nature poems) or senryu (haiku format, any subject matter).

Find Out More

about Haiku on the Internet.

67

Fall is bright yellow red
trees are bare, bark so cold
piles of maple leaves

—Josh Kleinhans, 4th grader, 2000

68

Two geese flying fast.
Breezy mists float below them.
Spring is coming soon.

—Angela Pomykaj, 5th grader, 2001

69

This is not the moon,
Nor is this the spring,
Of other springs,
And I alone
Am still the same.

—Ariwara No Narihira

70

A wild sea—
In the distance,
Over Sado,
The Milky Way.

—Bashó

71

The cicada sings
In the rotten willow.
Antares, the fire star,
Rolls in the west.

—Anonymous

72

Bears eating bacon
Outside my cousin's cabin.
Nobody got hurt.

—Erica Bilodeau, 5th grader, 2002

73

Heavy humid air
Water trickling slowly
Clear icy creek.

—Nathaniel Peterson, 5th grader, 2003

74

Joyful, bright blue sky
On the dock in the gold sun
Cute baby gator.

—Paige Allen, 5th grader, 2002

75

A violet bloomed
Casting beauty all around it
Adding to the world.

—Rachel Moger-Reischer

76

I'm Nobody! Who are you?

I'm Nobody! Who are you?
Are you—Nobody—too?
Then there's a pair of us!
Don't tell! they'd advertise—you know!
How dreary—to be—Somebody!
How public—like a Frog—
To tell your name—the livelong June—
To an admiring **Bog**!

—Emily Dickinson

Key Vocabulary

bog: marsh, swamp

Link

"The Railway Train" (105)

Invite students to create a short poem that focuses on an aspect of this poem. The poem might answer the poet's question: "Who are you?" or offer an opinion on whether or not it is "dreary to be somebody."

77

A Thought

Turn your ideas inside out,
And see if maybe
They don't make more sense
Than they originally did.

—Rachel Moger-Reischer

Find Out More

about the poet in *Emily Dickinson* (Bloom's Major Poets) by Harold Bloom, Chelsea House Publications, 1999, or in other sources; and in *The Complete Poems of Emily Dickinson*, Little, Brown, 1976.

78

My Quilt

As I look at the old patchwork quilt on
    my bed,
I remember what my old
grandmother said.
After she gave this quilt to me,
she told me a tale from over the sea.
A tale told when her grandma was
    young,
a tale that many times has been sung,
a tale of a baby wrapped up in rags,
that the farmer used as potato bags,
that the stable boy used for the sheep
    as bedding,
that the housewife used till her cats
    stopped shedding,
that little boys propped up on sticks as
    play huts,
that the doctor used to clean out cuts,
that the soldiers used when they
    practiced to shoot,
that the lumberjacks used to line their
    boots,
that a young washer woman came by,
while they were hung on the line to
    dry,
that she sewed into a quilt for her
    daughter, so cold,
while she told the tale of the rags so
    old.
The tale my grandmother told to me,
the tale from over, over the sea.

—Lauren Strainge
5th grader, 2001

79 | Soup

I saw the famous man eating soup.
I say he was lifting a fat broth
Into his mouth with a spoon.
His name was in the newspapers that day
Spelled out in tall black headlines
And thousands of people were talking about him.

When I saw him,
He sat bending his head over a plate
Putting soup in his mouth with a spoon.

—Carl Sandburg

Links

"Evening in Margaret's
Kitchen" (83),
"Charlotte" (142)

Springboard

Discuss the details the poets
use in "Soup," "Evening in
Margaret's Kitchen," and
"Charlotte" to describe the
subjects of their poems. Note
that in each poem the person
is described doing something
very ordinary (eating soup,
standing/dreaming, picking
flowers). Invite students to
write a poem describing a
person they observed doing
something very ordinary.

80 | Evening in Margaret's Kitchen

For Margaret Button Williams

Her silver rings, her liquid laugh, her sea blue gaze
Margaret stands at the window
Dreaming of younger days—
At 18 wreathed in ribbons, laced in lily white—
Margaret at evening remembers
Margaret in moonlight.

—Susan Moger

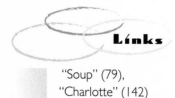

Links

"Soup" (79),
"Charlotte" (142)

81

You . . . and Your Dad

Traveling the interstate routes
With no sense of direction
Following no road map
Traveling only by the lay of the land
Going on only because
Of the love of the land

You and your dad

You, a curly-haired toddler
Without even the knowledge
To put the right shoes on the right feet
Listening to Willie Nelson in a trance

You
Your dad

Feeling the love, but not really
understanding it
Your bottle in one hand
The other, clutching the seat belt
Anticipating the next fork in the road

You, a rosy-cheeked kid

Not knowing anything but
Willie Nelson's voice and
The indescribable landscape
Not knowing
That later on in life you wish you would be
able to relive
That single moment
A thousand times
Only the hazy memory
Sticking to you like the apple juice leaking
from the bottle
Stuck to your lively little fingers at one time

You and your dad

On the interstate routes.

—Katie Ferman, age 11, 2004

Springboard

After reading this poem, ask students to write about a trip they
took with a parent or other family member at a very young age.
Have them start by brainstorming early memories. They might
choose to write about traveling to a nearby grocery store or
visiting a relative. Tell students that the poem can be very short.

82 To My Dear and Loving Husband

If ever two were one then surely we.
If ever man were loved by wife, then **thee**;
If ever wife were happy in a man,
Compare with me, **ye** women, if you can.
I prize thy love more than whole mines of gold
Or all the riches that the East doth hold.
My love is such that rivers cannot **quench**,
Nor aught but love from thee give **recompense**.
Thy love is such I can no way repay,
The heavens reward thee **manifold**, I pray.
Then while we live, in love let's so **persevere**
That when we live no more, we may live **ever**.

—Anne Bradstreet

Key Vocabulary

thee: you, one person
ye: you (plural)
quench: put out a fire
recompense: repay
manifold: many
persevere: continue
ever: forever

Key Vocabulary

whenas: when
methinks: I think
liquefaction: turning into a liquid
taketh: takes, appeals to

Springboard

Ask students to identify the words that add a sense of movement in this poem. What sounds in the first stanza suggest the flowing quality of Julia's clothes?

83 Upon Julia's Clothes

Whenas in silks my Julia goes,
Then, then (**methinks**) how sweetly flows
That **liquefaction** of her clothes.

Next, when I cast mine eyes, and see
That brave vibration each way free,
O how that glittering **taketh** me!

—Robert Herrick

84

Jump

Standing on that wall
"Jump, jump," everyone cried.
I can hear that voice run through my head,
Decide, decide, decide.

All that dark clear water
Brushing by my side,
My whole body yelling,
Decide, decide, decide!

"My cousin said, "If I jump,
you have to do it, too."
"All right," I answered, but I lied,
Once she jumped, again it was,
Decide, decide, decide.

My legs just wouldn't do it
It must be the bones inside.
I started to, but then I stopped,
Decide, decide, decide.

I decided not to jump
And we continued our raft ride.
Still that voice rings through my head,
Decide, decide, decide.

—Caitlin Peterson, 4th grader, 2000

Link

"The Road Not Taken"
(117)

Springboard

Make sure students
understand what the poet
had to decide to do or not
do. Then discuss why they
think the poet still hears
"that voice" saying "decide,
decide, decide." Ask students
to write a poem about a
decision they had to make
using the refrain "decide,
decide, decide." Compare the
decision in this poem to that
of Frost in "The Road Not
Taken."

85

Song for the Last Unicorn

Do you believe in unicorns?
Magical and free,
With silver wonder in their eyes,
With golden horns that hypnotize,
And spirits wild as the sea!

Do you believe in unicorns?
Mystical as night,
As shining as the moon above,
As soft as snow, as strong as love,
Elusive as starlight!

Where are all the unicorns?
Vanished, it is true,
But if your heart is pure and kind,
Just look inside, and you may find
One waiting there for you.

—Carol Peck

Key Vocabulary

mystical: mysterious, supernatural

86

Waiting for [You

For Ben

The house, wings folded, waits for you
In the darkened room my books are sailing
On shelves that vibrate gently.
The shelves reflect the builder;
But in my books I see myself.
And the house, waiting for you,
Sings under its breath.

—Susan Moger

87

Feelings Alive

When I'm happy, I'm like a big, red balloon,
When I'm excited, I'm like a rocket roaring to
     the moon
  And I soar way up in the blue!
But when I'm grumpy, I'm like an old
     wrinkled prune
And when I'm sad, I'm like a flute with
     no tune;
  It's okay to feel that way too—
There are all kinds of feelings in you!

When I'm calm, I'm like a peaceful sea,
When I'm brave, I'm like a big oak tree
  Standing tall and true;
But when I'm nervous, I'm like a hopping
     flea
And when I'm angry, I'm like a stinging bee;
  It's okay to feel that way, too—
  There are all kinds of feelings in you!

—Carol Peck

Link

"I Am Cherry Alive" (93)

Springboard

Discuss the poet's use of concrete images to describe feelings. Then have students describe how they feel when they are "happy, excited, calm, nervous, angry." Encourage them to expand these images into a poem using the phrases, "When I'm [a feeling] ... I'm like [a concrete image]." Compare the feelings expressed in this poem to the feelings expressed in "I Am Cherry Alive."

88 Brother in Hospital

Brother
In hospital
        Fevers, pain, broken leg,
Sleepy, hard to breathe, shots
        I.V.s
Get Well

— Vanessa Cooke, 5th grader, 2001

Links

"The American Flag" (2),
"Insects" (34)

Springboard

Explain that this poem is a cinquain
(like "The American Flag" and
"Insects"). Using information in the
Introduction on page 14, give students
some background about the form and
then ask them to write their own
cinquains about a person they know.

89 Aunts & Uncles

Three of my aunts—Hedwig, Harriet, and Flo
Had names that sound old-fashioned now, I know.

Their husbands' names were Irving, Al, and John—
Names are hooks to hang our memories on.

Aunt Flo worked hard but always had a smile
And offered a broad lap where I could sit a while.

Aunt Hedwig's cookies came out crisp and sweet
She kept our Nana's house, and hers, so very neat.

Aunt Harriet taught reading. She'd say, "Look!
I know you love to read; here's a new book."

Uncles Al and Irv and John were men who knew
a million funny jokes; great card games, too.

Saying their names unlocked my heart today
And let my memories come out to play.

— Susan Moger

90

Pine Bedding

On Saturday mornings
I clean
My guinea pig's cage
She'll squeak and holler
Like a maniac
I dump out the dirty bedding
Into a bag
And tie it up
But before
I put the fresh, new pine bedding in
The smell makes me remember that cold
afternoon
When I came home
When I had a bunny
Named Celia
Who walked instead of hopped
That day I ran to her cage
Behind the garage
I stopped and froze
The cage was tipped over
I suppose a dog or coyote did it
Celia was lying there lifeless
Now when I get upset
I pick up Sugar
and she'll breathe in my ear
As if she's saying
It's all right,
I'm still here.

—Whitney Fairchild, 5th grader, 2003

Springboard

Invite students to write a poem in which they express feelings through precise details about caring for a pet.

91

My Valentine

I will make you **brooches** and toys for your delight
Of bird song at morning and starshine at night
I will make a palace fit for you and me,
  Of green days in forests
  And blue days at sea.

—Robert Louis Stevenson

Key Vocabulary

brooches: pieces of
  jewelry that can be
  pinned to a jacket or
  dress

92

The First Time Anyone Called You My Boyfriend

Bobby's father took us to the movies
There were six of us,
Counting Bobby's father.
Everyone got popcorn—
Bobby's father paid.
When we sat down, you were on the aisle
I was six seats in.
After the movie started, I tried to see
If you were trying to look at me.
"Watch the movie, not your boyfriend,"
Bobby's father said.

—Susan Moger

93

I Am Cherry Alive

"I am cherry alive," the little girl sang,
"Each morning I am something new:
I am apple, I am plum, I am just as excited
As the boys who made the Hallowe'en bang:
I am tree, I am cat, I am blossom too:
When I like, if I like, I can be someone new,
Someone very old, a witch in a zoo:
I can be someone else whenever I think who,
And I want to be everything sometimes too:
And the peach has a pit and I know that too,
And I put it in along with everything
To make the grown-ups laugh whenever I sing:
And I sing: It is true; It is untrue;
I know, I know, the true is untrue,
The peach has a pit,
The pit has a peach:
And both may be wrong
When I sing my song,
But I don't tell the grown-ups: because it is sad,
And I want them to laugh just like I do
Because they grew up
And forgot what they knew
And they are sure
I will forget it someday too.
They are wrong. They are wrong.
When I sang my song, I knew, I knew!
I am red, I am gold,
I am green, I am blue,
I will always be me,
I will be always new!"

—Delmore Schwartz

Link

"Feelings Alive" (87)

Springboard

Discuss what the poet means in the last line of this poem, "I will always be new!" Compare the feelings expressed in this poem to the feelings expressed in "Feelings Alive."

94 Sea Shell

Sea Shell, Sea Shell,
Sing me a song, O Please!
A song of ships, and sailor men,
And parrots, and tropical trees,
Of islands lost in the **Spanish Main**
Which no man ever may find again,
Of fishes and corals under the waves,
And seahorses stabled in great green caves.
Sea Shell, Sea Shell,
Sing of the things you know so well.

—Amy Lowell

Key Vocabulary

Spanish Main: oceans controlled by Spain long ago

95 September

I already know where Africa is
and I already know how to
count to ten and
I went to school every day last year,
why do I have to go again?

—Lucille Clifton

96 Morning Memory

The smell of sweet morning
    when nobody is out
    and the sun is rising.
Reminds me of where I was born,
Reminds me of Puerto Rico
    where my family is.

—Ubec Aymat, 5th grader, 2001

Springboard

Have students write a short poem that starts with a sense (seeing, smelling, tasting, hearing, touching) and ends with "reminds me of . . ."

97

How Many Ways to Say Rhode Island

Swimming in the ocean
Having lots of fun
Splashing in the water
Through the sand we run
Coming home from the beach
After swimming many hours
Fighting over who will get
The first and hottest shower

Walking to the pond
Speeding on the boat
Feel the water splashing
Man, do I get soaked

Driving to the clam flats
Digging with my feet
Hope we get a lot of clams
From a yummy dinner to eat
Fishing on the rocks
and catching mostly trout

Enjoying my vacation
That's what Rhode Island's all about!

—Michaela Palmer, 5th grader, 2001

Link

"How Many Ways to Say Cooking" (120)

Springboard

Have students write a "How Many Ways to Say ..." poem, this time about a favorite place.

98 Song for a Little House

I'm glad our house is a little house,
   Not too tall nor too wide:
I'm glad the **hovering** butterflies
   Feel free to come inside.
Our little house is a friendly house.
   It is not shy or vain;
It gossips with the talking trees,
   And makes friends with the rain.
And quick leaves cast a **shimmer** of green
   Against our whited walls,
And in the **phlox**, the **dutious** bees
   Are paying duty **calls**.

—Christopher Morley

Key Vocabulary

hovering: floating
shimmer: sparkling light
phlox: an erect or trailing plant
   bearing lots of small flowers
dutious: dutiful, obedient
calls: visits

Link

"City" (101),
"Grandma Mountain" (107)

Springboard

Have students identify personification in this poem and in "Grandma Mountain" (107) and "City" (101). How do the poets achieve it? What words do they use to give a house, a mountain, and a city human qualities?

99 Schools

I learned to ride a bike
and go where the wind blows
I learned to row a boat
And dive through rainbows
In school I watch the clock
Until the bell rings
I've learned that I learn best
Out where the bird sings.

—Susan Moger

100 Broadway

This is the quiet hour; the theaters
Have gathered in their crowds, and steadily
The million lights blaze on for few to see,
Robbing the sky of stars that should be hers.
A woman waits with bag and shabby furs,
A **somber** man drifts by, and only we
Pass up the street unwearied, warm and free,
For over us the olden magic stirs.
Beneath the liquid splendor of the lights
We live a little **ere** the charm is spent;
This night is ours, of all the golden nights,
    The pavement an enchanted palace floor,
And Youth the player on the **viol**, who sent
    A **strain** of music through an open door.

—Sara Teasdale

Key Vocabulary

somber: dark, sad
ere: before
viol: stringed instrument
strain: a few notes of a tune

Link

"City" (101)

Springboard

Have students compare the way this poet describes a city scene to Langston Hughes's description in the poem "City" (101). Which poet uses personification?

Link

"Broadway" (100)

Springboard

Have students write a poem describing a contrast between morning and night in a familiar place, such as a playground, the school, or a basketball court where people play under the lights.

101 City

In the morning the city
Spreads its wings
Making a song
In stone that sings.

In the evening the city
Goes to bed
Hanging lights
About its head.

—Langston Hughes

102   Home Thoughts, from Abroad

O, to be in England
Now that April's there,
And whoever wakes in England
Sees, some morning, unaware,
That the lowest boughs and the brushwood **sheaf**
Round the elm-tree **bole** are in tiny leaf,
While the **chaffinch** sings on the orchard bough
In England—now!

And after April, when May follows,
And the whitethroat builds, and all the swallows!
Hark, where my blossom'd pear-tree in the hedge
Leans to the field and scatters on the clover
Blossoms and dewdrops—at the bent spray's edge—
That's the wise thrush; he sings each song twice over,
Lest you should think he never could recapture
The first fine careless rapture!
And though the fields look rough with **hoary** dew,
All will be gay when noontide wakes anew
The buttercups, the little children's **dower**
—Far brighter than this gaudy melon-flower!

—Robert Browning

Key Vocabulary

sheaf: bundle of leaves
bole: trunk of a tree
chaffinch: small,
  reddish-brown bird
hoary: white or gray
dower: gift

Find Out More

about Robert Browning in *Robert Browning* (Bloom's Major Poets) by Harold Bloom, Chelsea House Publications, 2000, or in other sources.

103 Roadways [Excerpt]

One road leads to London,
  One road leads to Wales,
My road leads me seawards
To the white dipping sails.
One road leads to the river,
And it goes singing slow;
My road leads to shipping,
Where the bronzed sailors go.
Leads me, **lures** me, calls me
  To salt green tossing sea;
A road without earth's road-dust
  Is the right road for me. . . .

—John Masefield

Key Vocabulary

lures: attracts, appeals to

Link

"Sea Fever" (140)

Springboard

Ask: "What road is a 'road without earth's dust'?" Why do you think the poet prefers that road?

104 Rhyme of the Rail

(Excerpt)

Singing through the forests,
  Rattling over ridges,
Shooting under arches,
  Rumbling over bridges,
Whizzing through the mountains,
  Buzzing **o'er** the **vale**,—
Bless me! this is pleasant,
  Riding on the Rail!

—John Godfrey Saxe

Key Vocabulary

o'er: over
vale: valley

105 The Railway Train

I like to see it lap the Miles—
And lick the Valleys up—
And stop to feed itself at Tanks—
And then—**prodigious** step

Around a Pile of Mountains—
And **supercilious peer**
In Shanties—by the sides of Roads—
And then a Quarry **pare**

To fit its Ribs
And crawl between
Complaining all the while
In horrid—hooting **stanza**—
Then chase itself down Hill—

And neigh like **Boanerges**—
Then—punctual as a Star
Stop—docile and **omnipotent**
At its own stable door—

—Emily Dickinson

Key Vocabulary

prodigious: amazing
supercilious: snobbish, superior
peer: look in
pare: cut down
stanza: section of a poem or song
Boanerges: loud-voiced speaker
omnipotent: all-powerful

Springboard

Have students identify the ways in which the poet personifies the train.

106 If I Were a Pony

If I were a pony,
A spotted pinto pony,
A racing, running pony
I would run away from school.
And I'd gallop on the mesa,
And I'd eat on the mesa,
And I'd sleep on the mesa,
And I'd never think of school.

—Navajo Students at Tohatchi School, New Mexico

Springboard

Challenge students to try writing "If I were/I would" poems like this one.

107

Grandma Mountain

Gray and white hair, like cotton
to her shoulders,
silky and soft blowing in the wind.

Stiff and tall she reaches for the sky.
When she welcomes you
she curtsies like a dancer.

When she curtsies she picks up her
beautiful white dress
sparkling in the sunlight
She is very pretty
like she always has been.

Grandma Mountain is strong and
powerful,
but kind in every way.
She listens, she watches
and she talks to me every day.

—Abby Brooking, 5th grader, 2002

Links

"Fog" (52), "City" (101),
"The Railway Train" (105)

Springboard

Have students identify the
ways in which the poet
personifies the mountain in
this poem. Encourage
children to read other
poems in which
personification is used
effectively (see Links above)
and then have them write
their own poem using this
imaginative figure of speech.

108

A Satisfactory Way
to Rule the World

Key Vocabulary

fancy: imagination

Twist everyone's words
To suit your **fancy**,
And the world will
Go on to please you.

—Rachel Moger-Reischer

109

The Great Figure

Among the rain
and lights
I saw the figure 5
in gold
on a red
firetruck
moving tense
unheeded
to gong clangs
siren howls
and wheels rumbling
through the dark city.

—William Carlos Williams

Key Vocabulary

unheeded: unnoticed

110

Sea Slant

On up the sea slant,
On up the horizon,
The ship limps.
The bone of her nose fog-gray,
The heart of her sea-strong,
She came a long way,
She goes a long way.
On up the sea slant,
On up the horizon,
She limps sea-strong, fog-gray
She is a green-lit night gray.
She comes and goes in sea-fog.
Up the horizon slant she limps.

—Carl Sandburg

Link

"On the Mississippi" (46)

Springboard

Compare the details the poet uses in describing the ship in this poem with the details Garland uses in "On the Mississippi."

Good Night

111

Many ways to say good night.

Fireworks at a pier on the Fourth of July
spell it with red wheels and yellow spokes.
They fizz in the air, touch the water and quit.
Rockets make a **trajectory** of gold-and-blue and then go out.

Railroad trains at night
spell with a smokestack mushrooming a white pillar.

Steamboats turn a curve in the Mississippi
Crying in a **baritone**
that crosses lowland cottonfields to **razorback** hill.

It is easy to spell good night.
     Many ways to spell good night.

—Carl Sandburg

Key Vocabulary

trajectory: path of a moving object
baritone: deep voice
razorback: sharp, ridged

Springboard

Have students write a poem that begins "Many ways to say/spell," followed by a common word or phrase. Encourage them to use the same range of imagery as Sandburg does in this poem.

Link

"Piano Lessons" (113)

Springboard

Challenge students to memorize this poem and act it out (in gestures) for an audience of younger children. For example, for the last line they can position their hands to look like a butterfly.

Our Clever Hands

112

Our clever hands can comb our hair
Or help us draw a perfect square;
They lift our ice cream for a lick
And even do arithmetic.

Our clever hands can strike a match
Or send our soda down the hatch;
They say hello and wave goodbye
And even make a butterfly!

—Carol Peck

113 Piano Lessons (Excerpt)

. . . I am learning to play
"It Might As Well Be Spring"
but my left hand would rather be jingling
the change in the darkness of my pocket
or taking a nap on an armrest.
I have to drag him into the music
like a difficult and neglected child.
This is the revenge of the one who never gets
to hold the pen or wave good-bye,
and now, who never gets to play the **melody**.

—Billy Collins

Key Vocabulary

melody: tune

Link

"Our Clever Hands" (112)

Springboard

With students compare this poem to "Our Clever Hands" and discuss details that Collins uses to describe his left hand and the details about both hands in Peck's poem. Talk about handedness and ambidexterity. Instruct students to write a poem in which both hands are equally useful.

114 Music

I hear music
rumbling trash cans
hammers hammering
books shutting pencils tapping
music—it's all around!

—Caitlin Mahar, 5th grader, 2001

Springboard

Challenge students to write their own poems that start "I hear music . . ."

115 | Shirt

My shirt is a **token** and symbol,
more than a cover for sun and rain,
my shirt is a signal,
and a teller of souls.
I can take off my shirt and tear it,
and so make a ripping razzly noise,
and the people will say,
"Look at him tear his shirt."
I can keep my shirt on.
I can stick around and sing like a little bird
and look 'em all in the eye and never be **fazed**.
I can keep my shirt on.

—Carl Sandburg

Key Vocabulary

token: sign
fazed: bothered

Springboard

Ask students: "How does the poet express his feeling of independence in this poem?" Have students write a poem about an article of clothing that they feel expresses something about themselves. As in Sandburg's poem, it could be a shirt.

116 | With an Encyclopedia You Can

Springboard

Have students look up several articles in a current encyclopedia and incorporate the titles into a poem.

Identify a butterfly
Understand a Roman Road
Tell one bird from the others
Make an ant house; see a toad.

See what makes the tides rise up
Find out who drinks tea
Compare the highest mountain
To the deepest sea.

—Susan Moger

The Road Not Taken

117

Two roads **diverged** in a yellow **wood**,
And sorry I could not travel both
And be one traveler, long I stood
And looked down one as far as I could
To where it bent in the undergrowth;

Then took the other, as just as **fair**
And having perhaps the better claim,
Because it was grassy and wanted wear;
Though as for that, the passing there
Had worn them really about the same,

And both that morning equally lay
In leaves no step had **trodden** black
Oh, I kept the first for another day!
Yet knowing how **way leads on to way**,
I doubted if I should ever come back.

I shall be telling this with a sigh
Somewhere ages and ages **hence**:
Two roads diverged in a wood, and I—
I took the one less traveled by,
And that has made all the difference.

—Robert Frost

Key Vocabulary

diverged: separated
wood: woods, forest
fair: pretty, attractive
trodden: walked on
way leads on to way:
  one road (way) leads to
  another
hence: from now

Link

"Jump" (84)

Springboard

Have students describe the two roads in the poem in their own words. Ask which road they would choose and why. Compare their choices to the one the poet made. Was he happy about his decision? Compare the poet's decision in this poem to the one the poet faced in "Jump." Have students write a poem about a choice they once made, including their feelings about the outcome.

118 Reading an Old Cookbook

1. Do You Have a Recipe for Spelling?
"Cold" slaw dressing, green tomato "pickel"
The ladies who wrote this cookbook
Could not spell worth a nickel!

2. Why?
Breaded turnip casserole
Codfish roast
Pepper noodle dinner
Bacon creamed on toast
Tutti Frutti Marlow
Dinner-in-a-pie
My question for these cooks is:
Why? Why? Why?

3. Cookies, Cakes, & Candies
Hermits, cheese rings, pecan macaroons
Walnut wafers, date bars, I'll be back real soon!
Brick cake, banana cake, cinnamon flats
Plain cake, pumpkin cake, hold on to your hats!
Haystacks, penuchi, peanut butter fudge
Sea foam, pineapple squares—I can't budge!

—Susan Moger

Links

"How Many Ways to Say Cooking" (120), "Fried Dough" (121)

Springboard

Consider this poem along with the food poems on the next page. Discuss the specific details that make "Fried Dough" so effective. Have students list foods they either like or dislike and then write a poem on one of the following topics: cooking with a relative or friend, sharing a meal or a snack with a friend, eating alone.

119 On Laughter

Laughter is full.
Spreading over a group,
Or secret, alone.

—Rachel Moger-Reischer

120

How Many Ways to Say Cooking

Smelly, yucky, gooey, chunky,
easy baking, try making,
fun tasting as you're baking,
cookie, cookie, crunch, crunch
yummy, yummy, munch, munch
taste good, taste bad
if you have it you'll be glad
taste the fun
taste the blast
taste it while it lasts.

—Kiki Camerota, 5th grader, 2001

Links

"How Many Ways to Say Rhode Island" (97), "Reading an Old Cookbook" (118), "Fried Dough" (121)

Springboard

Instruct students to write a "How Many Ways to Say [my favorite/least favorite food]" poem.

Link

"How Many Ways to Say Cooking" (120)

Springboard

Ask students to write a list of associations with a particular taste or smell. Encourage them to shape the results into a poem.

121

Fried Dough

The smell of fried dough reminds me
  of Lebanon Valley Speedway.
Engines starting up,
  race cars flying around the track,
Eating fried dough, watching my Dad
Race the 518 modified race car.

—Taylor Sheldon, 5th grader, 2003

122

Contrast

Cold is the snow,
Yet warm is the fire.
Cold is sorrow,
Yet warm is happiness.
Cold are the hearts of some,
Yet warm are the hearts of many.
Cold is grief,
Yet warm is friendship.
Cold is anger,
Yet warm is music.
Cold is war,
Yet warm is compassion.
Cold is bitterness,
Yet warm are tears.
Cold is frustration,
Yet warm is success.
Cold is **anguish**,
Yet warm are memories.
Cold is pain,
Yet warm is life.

—Rachel Moger-Reischer

Key Vocabulary

anguish: deep sadness

123

Problems, Problems!

If the sky falls,
Sweep up the pieces and get out your
watercolors;
If you are late to school,
Zap all their clocks back one hour;
If your computer refuses to work,
Take away its allowance for a week;
If your dog gets fleas,
Teach them to dance and sing;
If your crown keeps slipping down over your
eyes,
Watch the world through rubies.

—Shirley Johannesen Levine

Springboard

Have students list a collection of problems like the one this poet has included in her poem. Then brainstorm a positive (sometimes zany) solution for each one.

124

In a Breath

What is flying on the wings of the wind?
What is running with the bolts of lightning?
What is marching in time with the thunder?
What is singing to the tune of the rain?
What is **flitting** lightly **o'er** the grass?
What is coming with the rising of the sun?
What is floating on the dreamy crescent of the moon?
What is hidden in every flower?
What is portrayed by every smile?
What is **steeped** in the heart of the tenderest?
What is present in even the sternest **countenance**?
What is glowing from the rosy cheeks of **radiant**
health?
What is behind the glazed eyes of the feverish?
What is in the covering of snow?
What is in the many colored leaves?
What is riding over the rippling meadows?
What is sailing o'er the rollicking seas?
What is soaring on the wings of the sea gull?
What is crawling with the wiggling worm?
What is raising the humble and humbling the proud?
What is singing through the voices of the birds?
What is wailing through the mouth of the babe?
What is shouting with the joy of the child?
What is weeping with the grieving, and yet
rejoicing with the joyful?
What is in the echo of the past and the promise of
the future?

—Rachel Moger-Reischer

Key Vocabulary

flitting: flying quickly back and forth
o'er: over
steeped: soaked into
countenance: face, facial expression
radiant: filled with light

Springboard

Encourage students to come up with possible answers to the questions posed by the poet in this poem.

Poems About Poetry and Words

125

Spelling Bee

It takes a good speller
to spell *cellar*,
separate, and *benefiting*;
not omitting
cemetery, *cataclysm*,
picknicker and *pessimism*.
And have you ever tried
innocuous, *inoculate*,
dessert, *deserted*, *desiccate*;
divide and *spied*,
gnat, *knickers*, *gnome*,
crumb, *crypt*, and *chrome*;
surreptitious, *supersede*,
delete, *dilate*, *impede*?

—David McCord

Springboard

Challenge students to learn
to spell these words and then
hold a spelling bee, using
these and other words you
have been studying.

126

Spelling Challenge

A Squabble met a Quibble in a spelling test one day.
Said the Squabble to the Quibble,
"So what's <u>your</u> problem, eh?"
"*–ible* and *–able*," cried the Quibble,
"deciding which to use!"
"Here's what I do," said the Squabble.
"I just close my eyes and choose!"

—Susan Moger

127 | The Poet Speaks

I know there seems to be
Little reason or rhyme
For poets who write of beauty
In such conflicting times . . .
But I am one of those who **strive** to **yield**,
Golden fruits, from stone fields.

—John Henrik Clarke

Key Vocabulary

strive: work hard
yield: grow, cultivate

128 | Without a Net

A poem should fly through the air
Fifty feet up
Grab the trapeze with one hand
Wave with the other

A poem should ride two horses
At the same time
Backwards
While swallowing a sword

A poem you don't forget:
Walks the high wire
Without a net

—Susan Moger

129 | AEIOU

Vowels are quite tasty
When you use them well
Sprinkle them on consonants—
Just see the words you'll spell!

—Susan Moger

130

Long Ago

Stories hung in the air like smoke from home fires
Stories rose up like good bread in a hot oven
Stories lit the night like fierce lightning
Stories fell softly like first snow.

—Susan Moger

131

Primer Lesson

Look out how you use proud words.
When you let proud words go, it is not easy to call them back.
They wear long boots, hard boots; they walk off proud; they
can't hear you calling—
Look out how you use proud words.

—Carl Sandburg

Links

"Fog" (52),
"Playful Words" (132)

132

Playful Words

What fun to play with words,
To clutter them up the page.
Then discover them arranged in
carefully crafted rows.
They march with that special rhythm.

—Shirley Johannesen Levine

Link

"Primer Lesson" (131)

133 Just-Right Vocabulary Pie

The dictionary's a useful tool
My mother said to me
But if you want the perfect word
Climb the thesaurus tree!

The fruits in that tree are easy to see
(To observe, eyeball, espy)
Pick, choose, select, then bake
In a just-right vocabulary pie!

—Susan Moger

Springboard

Discuss with students the purpose of a thesaurus. Then challenge them to expand their vocabulary by looking up several everyday words in a thesaurus. When students are finished, encourage them to use the words in an original poem.

134 Hyperbole

My refrigerator's as humongous as a hippo
It's been filled for four billion years,
The cheese is as green as grass in all the world
It smells as bad as a fish that's been dead for twenty-three years,
The crackers are as soggy as if they'd been dipped in the ocean,
The ice cream melted last summer and turned into water
    with blue-green algae,
Only the toads wanted the old tofu, so we called it toad-food.

—Roy Moger-Reischer

Springboard

Challenge students to define hyperbole based on this poem (and with the help of a dictionary). Then ask them to write a poem with hyperbole in every line.

135 Synonyms

Claptrap, bombast, rodomontade
hogwash, jargon, and rant
blarney, nonsense, rigamarole
babble, prattle, and cant

—Susan Moger

Springboard

Encourage students to
incorporate other
synonyms into poems.

136 Onomatopoeia

It's hooshing!
It has four eyes.
When it is hungry, it goes "hisssss"!
When it sits down, it thuds.
It scratches!

—Roy Moger-Reischer

Link

"Jabberwocky" (168)

Springboard

Challenge student to define *onomatopoeia* based on
this poem (and with the help of a dictionary). Then ask
them to write a poem filled with onomatopoeia.
Compare "hooshing" in line 1 of this poem to some of
the made-up words in "Jabberwocky." Ask: "Can you
guess what any of these words mean?"

Poems of Beauty and Magic

137 Silver

Slowly, silently, now the moon
Walks the night in her silver **shoon**;
This way, and that, she peers, and sees
Silver fruit upon silver trees;
One by one the **casements** catch
Her beams beneath the silvery **thatch**;
Couched in his kennel, like a log,
With paws of silver sleeps the dog;
From their shadowy **cote** the white breasts peep
Of doves in a silver-feathered sleep;
A harvest mouse goes scampering by,
With silver claws and a silver eye;
And moveless fish in the water gleam,
By silver reeds in a silver stream.

—Walter de la Mare

Key Vocabulary

shoon: shoes
casements: window
  panes
thatch: roof
cote: shelter for birds

Link

"Velvet Shoes" (138)

Springboard

Ask students to describe the mood of this poem and to look at the ways the poet's repetition of *s* sounds at the beginning and end of certain words (for example, in *silver, peers, sees, sleeps, moveless,* and *stream*) contributes to the mood. Ask students to compare this poem to "Velvet Shoes." How are the two poems alike and different?

138

Velvet Shoes

Let us walk in the white snow
　　　In a soundless space;
With footsteps quiet and slow,
　　　At a **tranquil** pace,
　　　Under veils of white lace.

I shall go **shod** in silk,
　　　And you in wool,
White as white cow's milk,
　　　More beautiful
　　　Than the breast of a gull.

We shall walk through the still town
　　　In a windless peace;
We shall step upon white down,
　　　Upon silver fleece,
　　　Upon softer than these.

We shall walk in velvet shoes:
　　　Wherever we go
Silence will fall like dews
　　　On white silence below.
　　　We shall walk in the snow.

—Elinor Wylie

Key Vocabulary

tranquil: peaceful
shod: wearing shoes

Link

"Silver" (137)

Ask students: "What would velvet shoes feel like? How do the various 'touch' images in the poem contribute to a peaceful mood? How is this poem like 'Silver'? How is it different?"

139 The Children's Hour

Between the dark and the daylight,
When the night is beginning to **lower**,
Comes a pause in the day's occupations,
That is known as the Children's Hour.

I hear in the chamber above me
The **patter** of little feet,
The sound of a door that is opened,
And voices soft and sweet.

From my study I see in the lamplight,
Descending the broad hall stair,
Grave Alice, and laughing Allegra,
And Edith with golden hair.

A whisper, and then a silence:
Yet I know by their merry eyes
They are plotting and planning together
To take me by surprise.

A sudden rush from the stairway,
A sudden raid from the hall!
By three doors left unguarded
They enter my castle wall!

They climb up into my **turret**
O'er the arms and back of my chair;
If I try to escape, they surround me;
They seem to be everywhere.

They almost devour me with kisses,
Their arms about me **entwine**,
Till I think of the **Bishop of Bingen**
In his Mouse-Tower on the Rhine!

Do you think, o blue-eyed **banditti**,
Because you have scaled the wall,
Such an old mustache as I am
Is not a match for you all!

I have you fast in my fortress,
And will not let you depart,
But put you down into the dungeon
In the round-tower of my heart.

And there will I keep you forever,
Yes, forever and a day,
Till the walls shall crumble to ruin,
And **moulder** in dust away!

—Henry Wadsworth Longfellow

Key Vocabulary

lower: to get darker
patter: light, soft steps
turret: tower
entwine: wrap around
Bishop of Bingen: in a legend he was a villain attacked by mice
banditti: little bandits
moulder: decay

Springboard

Make sure students can visualize what is going on in this poem—the three girls and their father in the lamplit study just as night comes on. Have them identify the words the poet uses that evoke a military campaign carried out by the girls and their father's response.

Find Out More

about the poet in *Henry Wadsworth Longfellow: America's Beloved Poet* (World Writers) by Bonnie L. Lukes, Morgan Reynolds Publishing, 2002, or in other sources.

140

Sea Fever (Excerpt)

I must go down to the seas again, to the lonely sea and the sky,
And all I ask is a tall ship and a star to steer her by,
And the wheel's kick and the wind's song and the white sail's shaking,
And a gray mist on the sea's face, and a gray dawn breaking . . .

—John Masefield

Link

"Roadways" (103)

Springboard

With students, look at the alliteration (wheel, wind, white) in line 3 and the internal rhymes (all, tall) in line 2 and discuss how they propel the poem and make it rhythmic.

141

Fairy Land IV

Where the bee sucks, there suck I:
In a **cowslip**'s bell I lie;
There I **couch** when owls do cry.
On the bat's back I do fly
After summer merrily:
Merrily, merrily, shall I live now,
Under the blossom that hangs on the bough.

—William Shakespeare

Key Vocabulary

cowslip: yellow flower
couch: lie down

142

Charlotte

For Charlotte Anna Moore

Charlotte wears a sailor blouse
and a golden ring
When she's in the garden
We can hear her sing.
Right now she's picking peonies
Purple, pink, and white
She'll put them on the table
For our delight tonight.

—Susan Moger

Links

"Soup" (79), "Evening in Margaret's Kitchen" (80)

Springboard

See the activity suggested in "Soup," on page 64.

143

A Birthday Poem

Just past dawn, the sun stands
with its heavy red head
in a black **stanchion** of trees,
waiting for someone to come
with his bucket
for the foamy white light,
and then a long day in the pasture.
I too spend my days grazing,
feasting on every green moment
till darkness calls,
and with the others
I walk away into the night,
swinging the little tin bell
of my name.

—Ted Kooser

Key Vocabulary

stanchion: metal frame that holds cows for milking

Springboard

Explore the specific words that the poet uses to bring this extended image to life. To what is he comparing the sun and himself?

144

Chamber Music V

Lean out of the window,
Goldenhair,
    I hear you singing
A merry **air**.
    My book was closed,
I read no more,
    Watching the fire dance
On the floor.
    I have left my book,
I have left my room,
    For I heard you singing
Through the gloom.
    Singing and singing
A merry air,
    Lean out of the window,
Goldenhair.

—James Joyce

Key Vocabulary

air: song

Link

"Chamber Music XXXV" (45)

Springboard

Compare this poem to "Chamber Music XXXV," looking at the author's choice of words and rhythm which creates two very different moods.

145

Crows

Crows walk with stately stalking,
Stopping only for quick talking,
In tight black buckled bunches,
Eating their little lunches.
Notice sensible squawking,
Of stately stalking crows.

—Patricia Moger Varshavtchik

Springboard

Have students look closely at the imagery and sounds in this poem. Note that the "-alk" end rhyme resembles the "caw" sound of crows. Then ask students to carefully describe in six image-packed lines a bird or animal they have observed.

Friday Night at Miss Farida's Piano Lesson

146

Miss Farida loves
vanilla-smelling candles
which flicker
against the sleeping couch.
I place my sandals
beside the spill
of shoes and slippers **strewn**
across the plastic mat
in the hallway to her room.
I see the Sesame Street stickers propped
near the electric piano,
tangled in a hoop
of dreaming dust,
and the pedals, wrapped in a layer
of fine metal.
Miss Farida takes my stack
of weary books
that whimper as she turns to "Stepping Stones."
My delicate hands
look like tiny mice skittering
across the keys.
I play to a beat from the metronome
fast as a hummingbird's heartbeat,
slow as a whale's.

Miss Farida takes a pencil
from her hair and writes
in my notebook.
"Tonight you will write a song
about New Year's."
I pick up my denim
bag and dump
my books into it.
Already, I begin to hear
the notes of endless
possibilities for my composition:
The orchestra of 10,000
fuchsia fireworks exploding
in the air,
the symphony of sparklers,
the dropping ball of melody,
the score of the night,
filled with new beginnings.

—Tae Kathleen Keller,
age 8, 2003

Key Vocabulary

strewn: spread around
fuchsia: purplish red

Springboard

Ask the class what assignment Miss Farida gave to the poet and whether they think the student is up to the task. Challenge students to write a poem about a new year—it could be a calendar or a school year or another turning point in the year after which all will be new.

147

The Song of Wandering Aengus

I went out to the hazel wood,
Because a fire was in my head,
And cut and peeled a hazel wand,
And hooked a berry to a thread;
And when white moths were on the wing,
And moth-like stars were flickering out,
I dropped the berry in a stream
And caught a little silver trout.

When I had laid it on the floor
I went to blow the fire **aflame**,
But something **rustled** on the floor,
And some one called me by my name:
It had become a **glimmering** girl
With apple blossom in her hair
Who called me by my name and ran
And faded through the brightening air.

Though I am old with wandering
Through hollow lands and hilly lands,
I will find out where she has gone,
And kiss her lips and take her hands;
And walk among long **dappled** grass,
And **pluck** till time and times are done
The silver apples of the moon,
The golden apples of the sun.

—William Butler Yeats

Key Vocabulary

aflame: into a flame, on fire
rustled: made soft sounds
glimmering: shining with a dim light
dappled: spotted (as with sunlight)
pluck: pick

Link

"The Wild Swans at Coole" (48)

Springboard

Make sure students understand what "happens" in this poem. They should be aware of how magical the apparition is that appears. Compare the mood of this poem to "The Wild Swans at Coole" by the same author.

148

I Wandered Lonely as a Cloud

I wandered lonely as a cloud
That floats on high **o'er vales** and hills,
When all at once I saw a crowd,
A host, of golden daffodils;
Beside the lake, beneath the trees,
Fluttering and dancing in the breeze.

Continuous as the stars that shine
And twinkle on the Milky Way,
They **stretch'd** in never-ending line
Along the margin of a bay:
Ten thousand saw I at a glance,
Tossing their heads in sprightly dance.

The waves beside them danced; but they
Out-did the sparkling waves in **glee**:
A poet could not but be gay,
In such a **jocund** company:
I gazed—and gazed—but little thought
What wealth the show to me had brought:

For **oft**, when on my couch I lie
In vacant or in pensive mood,
They flash upon that inward eye
Which is the bliss of solitude;
And then my heart with pleasure fills,
And dances with the daffodils.

—William Wordsworth

Key Vocabulary

o'er: over
vales: valleys
stretch'd: stretched
glee: happiness
jocund: cheerful
oft: often

Link

"Daffadowndilly" (56)

Springboard

Ask the following questions: "What was the speaker's mood before he arrived at the scene described in the poem? How do you know? What was the scene he came upon? What effect does the 'show' (line 21) have on the speaker? What does he later realize?" Invite some students to illustrate this poem. Have others write a short poem about a startling scene they appreciated when they looked back on it later.

Find Out More

about the poet in *William Wordsworth* (Bloom's Major Poets) by Harold Bloom, Chelsea House Publications, 1998, or in other sources.

149

The Bells

Hear the **sledges** with the bells,
        Silver bells!
What a world of merriment their melody **foretells**!
        How they tinkle, tinkle, tinkle,
5   In the icy air of night!
        While the stars, that oversprinkle
        All the heavens, seem to twinkle
            With a **crystalline** delight;
        Keeping time, time, time,
10   In a sort of **Runic** rhyme,
To the **tintinnabulation** that so musically wells
        From the bells, bells, bells, bells,
            Bells, bells, bells—
From the jingling and the tinkling of the bells.

15   Hear the mellow wedding bells,
        Golden bells!
What a world of happiness their harmony foretells!
        Through the balmy air of night
        How they ring out their delight!
20   From the **molten**-golden notes,
            And all in tune,
        What a liquid **ditty** floats
To the turtle-dove that listens, while she **gloats**
            On the moon!
25   Oh, from out the sounding cells,
What a gush of **euphony voluminously** wells!
            How it swells!
            How it dwells
        On the Future! how it tells
30   Of the rapture that **impels**
        To the swinging and the ringing
        Of the bells, bells, bells,
        Of the bells, bells, bells, bells,
            Bells, bells, bells—
35   To the rhyming and the chiming of the bells!

Hear the loud **alarum** bells,

Brazen bells!

What a tale of terror, now, their **turbulency** tells!

In the startled ear of night

40 How they scream out their **affright**!

Too much horrified to speak,

They can only shriek, shriek,

Out of tune,

In a **clamorous** appealing to the mercy of the fire,

45 In a mad **expostulation** with the deaf and frantic fire,

Leaping higher, higher, higher,

With a desperate desire,

And a resolute endeavor

Now—now to sit or never,

50 By the side of the pale-faced moon.

Oh, the bells, bells, bells!

What a tale their terror tells

Of Despair!

How they clang, and clash, and roar!

55 What a horror they outpour

On the bosom of the **palpitating** air!

Yet the ear it fully knows,

By the twanging

And the clanging,

60 How the danger ebbs and flows;

Yet the ear distinctly tells,

In the jangling

And the wrangling,

How the danger sinks and swells,—

65 By the sinking or the swelling in the anger of the bells,

Of the bells,

Of the bells, bells, bells, bells,

Bells, bells, bells—

In the clamor and the **clangor** of the bells!

70 Hear the tolling of the bells,
    Iron bells!
What a world of solemn thought their **monody** compels!
   In the silence of the night
   How we shiver with affright
75 At the melancholy menace of their tone!
   For every sound that floats
   From the rust within their throats
    Is a groan.
  And the people—ah, the people,
80 They that dwell up in the steeple,
    All alone,
 And who tolling, tolling, tolling,
  In that muffled **monotone**,
  Feel a glory in so rolling
85 On the human heart a stone—
They are neither man nor woman,
They are neither brute nor human,
   They are Ghouls:
 And their king it is who tolls;
90 And he rolls, rolls, rolls,
   Rolls
  A **paean** from the bells;
 And his merry bosom swells
  With the paean of the bells,
95 And he dances, and he yells:
Keeping time, time, time,
In a sort of Runic rhyme,
  To the paean of the bells,
   Of the bells:
100 Keeping time, time, time,
In a sort of Runic rhyme,
To the throbbing of the bells,
Of the bells, bells, bells—

Key Vocabulary

sledges: sleds
foretells: predicts the future
crystalline: like glass
Runic: mysteriously, magically symbolic
tintinnabulation: ringing of bells
molten: melted
ditty: simple song
gloats: feels superior to
euphony: pleasing sound
voluminously: loudly
impels: drives forward
alarum: alarm
brazen: made of bronze
turbulency: storminess
affright: fear
clamorous: noisy
expostulation: strong demand
palpitating: trembling
clangor: loud ringing
monody: one voice singing
monotone: a single tone
paean: song of praise

Find Out More

about the poet in *Edgar Allan Poe* by Tom Streissguth, Lerner, 2001, or in other sources.

105 To the sobbing of the bells;
     Keeping time, time, time,
        As he knells, knells, knells,
     In a happy Runic rhyme,
     To the rolling of the bells,
        Of the bells, bells, bells:
110   To the tolling of the bells,
     Of the bells, bells, bells, bells,
        Bells, bells, bells—
     To the moaning and the groaning of the bells.

—Edgar Allan Poe

Links

"The Cataract at Lodore" (47),
"The Bells of Shandon" (151)

Springboard

Read the poem aloud, with students taking different parts. Discuss the many different moods bells express in this poem. Ask: "Which mood is described best?" Have students refer to specific lines of the poem in making their case.

Key Vocabulary

peculiar: strange

Springboard

This is a poem to read aloud and savor many times over. Discuss the images that make this poem so vivid. For example, the poet describes the "peculiar words" as "many-lettered, one-syllabled lumps, which I squeeze" and, through the magic of imagery, the words become blackberries. Create a bulletin board display of "peculiar words" students come across in their reading.

150

Blackberry Eating

I love to go out in late September
among the fat, overripe, icy, black blackberries
to eat blackberries for breakfast,
the stalks very prickly, a penalty
they earn for knowing the black art
of blackberry-making; and as I stand among them
lifting the stalks to my mouth, the ripest berries
fall almost unbidden to my tongue,
as words sometimes do, certain **peculiar** words
like *strengths* or *squinched*,
many-lettered, one-syllabled lumps,
which I squeeze, squinch open, and splurge well
in the silent, startled, icy, black language
of blackberry-eating in late September.

—Galway Kinnell

151

The Bells of Shandon (Excerpt)

With deep affection,
And recollection,
I often think of
   Those Shandon bells,
Whose sounds so wild would,
In the days of childhood,
Fling around my cradle
   Their magic spells.
On this I **ponder**
Where'er I wander,
And thus grow fonder,
   Sweet **Cork**, of **thee**;
With **thy** bells of Shandon,
That sound so grand on
The pleasant waters
   Of the River Lee.

I've heard bells chiming
Full many a **clime** in,
Tolling sublime in
   Cathedral shrine,
While at a **glib** rate
Brass tongues would vibrate—
But all their music
   Spoke **naught** like **thine**;
For memory, dwelling
On each proud swelling
Of the **belfry knelling**
   Its bold notes free,
Made the bells of Shandon
Sound far more grand on
The pleasant waters
   Of the River Lee. . . .

—Francis Mahony

Key Vocabulary

ponder: think about
Cork: a county and city in Ireland
thee: you
thy: your
clime: place on earth
glib: easy, infomal
naught: not at all
thine: yours
belfry: area in a tower where bells are hung
knelling: ringing

Links

"Onomatopoeia" (136), "The Bells" (149)

Springboard

Compare this poem to "The Bells." Have students decide which is the more effective at evoking the sounds of bells. Have students write poems about sounds in which they use onomatopoeia to convey the sound.

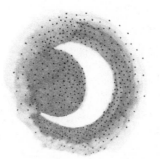

152

The Moon

After writing poems all day,
I go off to see the moon in the pines.
Far in the woods I sit down against a pine.
The moon has her porches turned to face the light,
But the deep part of her house is in the darkness.

—Robert Bly

153

We Are All Riders to the Sea

We are all riders to the sea,
Across the flat gray-green land,
Through forests **aisled** and steadfast,
Reaching sun-drenched, leaf-crowned
Branches to the sky.

To the sea—the salty, white-capped
Heaving mountains of the sea
Where the sun pours into blue
And the clouds balance the tongues of fog.

We ride wild gray horses barebacked
Clutching wind-tangled manes
Galloping the grass green miles away
Forever to the sea
Pulled by our own will
Forever washed in the white waves.

—Susan Moger

Key Vocabulary

aisled: planted in straight rows

154

Winter Blue

Water turns to ice.
The blue mailbox,
has been covered by snow.
The water is no longer blue,
now it's white.
Winter blue.

—Nate Dingman,
5th grader, 2002

Links

"Winter Blue" (154),
"Yellow" (156), "The
Color Yellow" (157)

Springboard

After students have read the color poems collected here, have them write some color poems of their own.

155

Lime Green

Lime green is dripping grass
   with clear water,
Wonderful parrots flying
swiftly over the rainforest.
Sweet limes in seltzer waiting
   to be drunk
Lime green is the greenest of
   frogs in my backyard.

—Sarah Heitzman, 5th grader, 2002

156

Yellow

Yellow,
Bananas ready and ripe
Sour lemons wait in the
      aisle,
Pineapples drift in juice,
Sweet lemonade quenches
      your thirst,
Butterscotch ice cream
Melts on your tongue,
Caramel chews fill your
Mouth with flavor,
The sun warms the planet
      our home,
Yellow leaves fall to the
      ground,
Dandelions refuse to stop
Growing in number,
Sunflowers reach for the
      sky,
Daffodils have a scent like
      no other,
Yellow.

—Dylan Sorenson,
5th grader, 2002

157

The Color Yellow

Yellow is big, booming, burning,
      crackling fireworks.
Yellow is the sound of popping
      buttery popcorn.
Yellow is the tart taste of lemons.
Yellow is bright, shocking
      lightning
Yellow is a small dandelion in a big field.

—Brendan Nixon, 5th grader, 2001

Poems for Fun

FOUR POEMS FROM *A CHILD'S GARDEN OF VERSES*

—Robert Louis Stevenson

158 Bed in Summer

In winter I get up at night
And dress by yellow candle-light.
In summer quite the other way,
I have to go to bed by day.
I have to go to bed and see
The birds still hopping on the tree,
Or hear the grown-up people's feet
Still going past me in the street.
And does it not seem hard to you,
When all the sky is clear and blue,
And I should like so much to play,
To have to go to bed by day?

159 At the Sea-side

When I was down beside the sea
A wooden spade they gave to me
To dig the sandy shore.
My holes were empty like a cup.
In every hole the sea came up,
Till it could come no more.

My Shadow

I have a little shadow that goes in and out with me,
And what can be the use of him is more than I can see.
He is very, very like me from the heels up to the head;
And I see him jump before me, when I jump into my bed.
The funniest thing about him is the way he likes to grow—
Not at all like proper children, which is always very slow;
For he sometimes shoots up taller like an **india-rubber** ball,
And he sometimes goes so little that there's none of him at all.
He hasn't got a notion of how children ought to play,
And can only make a fool of me in every sort of way.
He stays so close behind me, he's a coward you can see;
I'd think shame to stick to **nursie** as that shadow sticks to me!
One morning, very early, before the sun was up,
I rose and found the shining dew on every buttercup;
But my lazy little shadow, like an **arrant** sleepy-head,
Had stayed at home behind me and was fast asleep in bed.

Key Vocabulary

india rubber: rubber
nursie: live-in babysitter
arrant: complete

Rain

The rain is falling all around,
It falls on field and tree,
It rains on the umbrellas here,
And on the ships at sea.

Find Out More

about the poetry of Robert Louis Stevenson
in *A Child's Garden of Verses*.

162

Silly Supper Farm

The horse eats popcorn and the pigs eat snow,
The cows eat dewdrops and the ducks eat dough,
At suppertime on silly supper farm!

The calves eat spinach and the dogs eat ice,
The goats eat gumdrops and the chicks eat spice.
At suppertime on silly supper farm!

The mice eat dustballs and the doves eat clay,
The llamas eat toothpaste and the cats eat hay.
At suppertime on silly supper farm.

(The animals are starting
To view supper with alarm.
Can't *someone* change the menu here
At silly supper farm?)

—Susan Moger

Have students write
their own "silly
supper" or "beserk
breakfast" poems.

163

**Key
Vocabulary**

parasol: small umbrella
used for shade, not
protection from rain

When Fishes Set Umbrellas Up

When fishes set umbrellas up
If the rain-drops run,
Lizards will want their **parasols**
To shade them from the sun.

—Christina Rossetti

164

A Nautical Ballad (Excerpt)

A capital ship for an ocean trip
    Was *The **Walloping** Window-blind*—
No gale that blew dismayed her crew
    Or troubled the captain's mind.
The man at the wheel was taught to feel
    Contempt for the wildest blow,
And it often appeared, when the weather had cleared,
    That he'd been in his bunk below.
The **boatswain's mate** was very **sedate**,
    Yet fond of amusement, too;
And he played hop-scotch with the starboard watch,
    While the captain tickled the crew.
And the gunner we had was apparently mad,
    For he sat on the **after-rail**,
And fired salutes with the captain's boots,
    In the teeth of the booming gale.
The captain sat in a **commodore's** hat
    And dined, in a royal way,
On toasted pigs and pickles and figs
    And **gummery** bread, each day.
But the cook was Dutch, and behaved as such;
    For the food that he gave the crew
Was a number of tons of hot-cross buns,
    Chopped up with sugar and glue.
And we all felt ill as mariners will,
    On a diet that's cheap and rude;
And we shivered and shook as we dipped the cook
    In a tub of his **gluesome** food. . . .

—Charles Edward Carryl

Key Vocabulary

walloping: huge
contempt: scorn, disapproval
boatswain's mate: member of a ship's crew
sedate: serious
after-rail: the back of the ship
commodore: a naval officer
gummery: a made-up word
gluesome: like glue

Springboard

This is a song! Find the music and enjoy singing it with the class—accompanied or unaccompanied.

165 The Squirrel

Whisky Frisky,
Hippity Hop,
Up he goes
To the tree top!

Whirly, twirly,
Round and round,
Down he scampers
To the ground.

Furly, curly,
What a tail,
Tall as a feather,
Broad as a sail.

Where's his supper?
In the shell,
Snappy, cracky,
Out it fell.

—Anonymous

Springboard

Have students solve the riddle—what is the squirrel's supper?

Find Out More

about the origin of the word *squirrel*.

166 Mary's Lamb (Excerpt)

Mary had a little lamb,
    Its fleece was white as snow;
And everywhere that Mary went,
    The lamb was sure to go.

He followed her to school one day—
    That was against the rule;
It made the children laugh and play,
    To see a lamb at school.

So the teacher turned him out,
    But still he **lingered** near,
And waited patiently about,
    Till Mary did appear.

Then he ran to her, and laid
    His head upon her arm,
As if he said, "I'm not afraid—
    You'll keep me from all harm."

"What makes the lamb love Mary so?"
    The eager children cry.
"Oh, Mary loves the lamb, you know,"
    The teacher did reply. . . .

—Sara Josepha Hale

Key Vocabulary

lingered: waited around

Springboard

Students can recite this poem, or even act it out, in a presentation to a class of younger children.

167

The Owl and the Pussy-Cat

The owl and the Pussy-Cat went to sea
In a beautiful pea-green boat,
They took some honey, and plenty of money,
Wrapped up in a **five-pound note**.
The Owl looked up to the stars above,
And sang to a small guitar,
"O Lovely Pussy! O Pussy, my love
What a beautiful Pussy you are,
You are!
You are!
What a beautiful Pussy you are!"

Pussy said to the Owl, "You elegant **fowl**!
How charmingly sweet you sing!
O let us be married, too long we have **tarried**:
But what shall we do for a ring?"
They sailed away, for a year and a day,
To the land where the Bong-tree grows,
And there in a wood a Piggy-wig stood
With a ring at the end of his nose,
His nose,
His nose,
With a ring at the end of his nose.

"Dear Pig, are you willing to sell for one **shilling**
Your ring?" Said the Piggy, "I will."
So they took it away, and were married next day
By the Turkey who lives on the hill.
They dined on **mince**, and slices of **quince**,
Which they ate with a **runcible spoon**;
And hand in hand, on the edge of the sand,
They danced by the light of the moon,
The moon,
The moon,
They danced by the light of the moon.

—Edward Lear

Key Vocabulary

five-pound note: English paper money
fowl: bird
tarried: waited
shilling: old-fashioned English coin
mince: chopped food
quince: a sour fruit
runcible spoon: a 3-pronged fork with a cutting edge

Springboard

Invite the class to "act out" this poem with students taking the parts of the owl, the cat, and one or two narrators for the connecting verses. They could also illustrate the poem and present copies of their work to the school library or to a class of younger students.

168

Jabberwocky

'Twas brillig, and the slithy toves
   Did gyre and gimble in the wabe:
All mimsy were the borogoves,
   And the momeraths outgrabe.

"Beware the Jabberwock, my son!
   The jaws that bite, the claws that catch!
Beware the Jubjub bird, and shun
   The frumious Bandersnatch!"

He took his vorpal sword in hand:
   Long time the manxome foe he sought—
So rested he by the Tumtum tree,
   And stood awhile in thought.

And, as in uffish thought he stood,
   The Jabberwock, with eyes of flame,
Came whiffling through the tulgey wood,
   And burbled as it came!

One, two! One, two! And through and through
   The vorpal blade went snicker-snack!
He left it dead, and with its head
   He went galumphing back.

"And, has thou slain the Jabberwock?
   Come to my arms, my beamish boy!
O frabjous day! Callooh! Callay!"
   He chortled in his joy.

'Twas brillig, and the slithy toves
   Did gyre and gimble in the wabe;
All mimsy were the borogoves,
   And the momeraths outgrabe!

—Lewis Carroll

Springboard

Read students the following quote from *Through the Looking-Glass and What Alice Found There* in which Alice comments on this poem: "'It seems very pretty,' she said. . . , 'but it's rather hard to understand!' (You see she didn't like to confess even to herself, that she couldn't make it out at all.) 'Somehow it seems to fill my head with ideas—only I don't exactly know what they are! However, somebody killed something: that's clear, at any rate—'" Have students identify the adjectives, nouns, verbs, and rules of grammar within this (largely) made-up language.

Find Out More

about *Through the Looking-Glass and What Alice Found There* by Lewis Carroll. A Web site devoted to this poem is found at **http://www.jabberwocky.com**.

169

The Lobster-Quadrille

"Will you walk a little faster?" said a **whiting** to a snail,
"There's a porpoise close behind us, and he's treading on my tail.
See how eagerly the lobsters and the turtles all advance!
They are waiting on the **shingle**—will you come and join the dance?
Will you, won't you, will you, won't you, will you join the dance?
Will you, won't you, will you, won't you, won't you join the dance?
"You can really have no notion how delightful it will be
When they take us up and throw us, with the lobsters, out to sea!"
But the snail replied "Too far, too far!" and gave a look **askance**—
Said he thanked the whiting kindly, but he would not join the dance.
Would not, could not, would not, could not, would not join the dance.
Would not, could not, would not, could not, could not join the dance.
"What matters it how far we go?" his **scaly** friend replied.
"There is another shore, you know, upon the other side.
The further off from England the nearer is to France—
Then turn not pale, beloved snail, but come and join the dance.
Will you, won't you, will you, won't you, will you join the dance?
Will you, won't you, will you, won't you, won't you joint the dance?

—Lewis Carroll

Key Vocabulary

whiting: silvery fish
shingle: loose gravel made up of
   flattened pebbles and stones,
   found on beaches
askance: with a side glance
scaly: covered with scales

170 | Billy Button

Billy Button bought a buttered biscuit.
Did Billy Button buy a buttered biscuit?
If Billy Button bought a buttered biscuit,
Where's the buttered biscuit Billy Button bought?

—Anonymous

171 | Fuzzy Wuzzy

Fuzzy wuzzy was a bear
Fuzzy wuzzy had no hair
Fuzzy wuzzy wasn't fuzzy
Was he?

—Anonymous

172 | British Warm

Inspired by the brand name on a hot water bottle.

British warm and British cold.
British new and British old.
British drop and British hold.
British silver and British gold.
British clean and British mold.
British straight and British fold.
British hide and British behold.
British secret and British told.
British bought and British sold.
British bounced and British rolled.
British light and British bold.

—Roy Moger-Reischer

Springboard

Invite students to write a poem of several lines, using the same rhyme for the final syllable of each line (the way *—old* is used in this poem).

Casey at the Bat

173

The outlook wasn't brilliant for the **Mudville nine** that day;
The score stood four to two with but one inning more to play.
And then when Cooney died at first and Barrows did the same,
A sickly silence fell upon the **patrons** of the game.

5   A **straggling** few got up to go in deep despair. The rest
Clung to the hope which springs eternal in the human breast;
They thought if only Casey could but get a whack at that—
We'd put up even money now with Casey at the bat.

But Flynn preceded Casey, as did also Jimmy Blake,
10   And the former was a **lulu** and the latter was a **cake**,
So upon that stricken multitude grim **melancholy** sat,
For there seemed but little chance of Casey's getting to the bat.

But Flynn let drive a single, to the wonderment of all,
And Blake, the much despised, tore the cover off the ball;
15   And when the dust had lifted, and the men saw what had occurred,
There was Jimmy safe at second and Flynn a-hugging third.

Then from five thousand throats and more there rose a lusty yell;
It rumbled through the valley, it rattled in the **dell**;
It knocked upon the mountain and **recoiled** upon the flat,
20   For Casey, mighty Casey, was advancing to the bat.

There was ease in Casey's manner as he stepped into his place;
There was pride in Casey's bearing and a smile on Casey's face.
And when, responding to the cheers, he lightly **doffed** his hat,
No stranger in the crowd could doubt 'twas Casey at the bat.

25   Ten thousand eyes were on him as he rubbed his hands with dirt;
Five thousand tongues applauded when he wiped them on his shirt.
Then while the **writhing** pitcher ground the ball into his hip,
Defiance gleamed in Casey's eye, a **sneer** curled Casey's lip.

And now the leather-covered **sphere** came **hurtling** through the air,
30 And Casey stood a-watching it in **haughty grandeur** there.
Close by the sturdy **batsman** the ball **unheeded** sped—
"That ain't my style," said Casey. "Strike one," the umpire said.

From the benches, black with people, there went up a muffled roar,
Like the beating of the storm waves on a stern and distant shore.
35 "Kill him! Kill the umpire!" shouted someone on the stand;
And it's likely they'd have killed him had not Casey raised his hand.

With a smile of Christian charity great Casey's **visage** shone;
He stilled the rising **tumult**; he **bade** the game go on;
He signaled to the pitcher, and once more the **spheroid** flew;
40 But Casey still ignored it, and the umpire said, "Strike two!"

"Fraud!" cried the maddened thousand, and echo answered, "Fraud!"
But one scornful look from Casey and the audience was awed.
They saw his face grow stern and cold, they saw his muscles strain,
And they knew that Casey wouldn't let that ball go by again.

45 The sneer is gone from Casey's lip, his teeth are clenched in hate;
He pounds with cruel violence his bat upon the plate.
And now the pitcher holds the ball, and now he lets it go
And now the air is shattered by the force of Casey's blow.

Oh, somewhere in this favored land the sun is shining bright;
50 The band is playing somewhere, and somewhere hearts are light,
And somewhere men are laughing, and somewhere children shout,
But there is no joy in Mudville—mighty Casey has struck out.

—Ernest L. Thayer

Key Vocabulary

Mudville nine: Mudville baseball team (nine players)
patrons: people who came to see the game
straggling: hanging back
lulu and **cake:** old-fashioned slang for poor players
melancholy: sadness
dell: small valley
recoiled: pulled back
doffed: took off
'twas: it was
writhing: squirming, twisting in pain
defiance: standing up to someone, resistance
sneer: a scornful look
sphere: round object, baseball
hurtling: traveling fast
haughty: stuck-up, acting superior
grandeur: greatness
batsman: batter
unheeded: ignored
visage: face
tumult: excitement, shouting
bade: commanded
spheroid: round object, baseball

Springboard

Have students practice reading this poem aloud with maximum effect—there are enough lines for everyone to have a part. The last four lines are often quoted, so students could memorize them. Perform your class reading of this poem for invited families of the whole school to enjoy.

174 How Many Seconds?

How many seconds in a minute?
Sixty, and no more in it.
How many minutes in an hour?
Sixty for sun and shower.
How many hours in a day?
Twenty-four for work and play.
How many days in a week?
Seven both to hear and speak.
How many weeks in a month?
Four, as the swift moon **runneth**.
How many months in a year?
Twelve the **almanack** makes clear.
How many years in an age?
One hundred says the **sage**.
How many ages in time?
No one knows the rhyme.

—Christina Rossetti

Key Vocabulary

runneth: runs
almanack: a book published yearly with information about weather and current events
sage: a wise person

175 Road Trip

Got the map?
Want the front seat
Or the back?
Locked the door?
Stowed the snack?
One last thing I need to know:
Where to go!

—Susan Moger

176 Invitation

Party! Party! Whirl and twirl!
I'm the eight-year-old birthday girl!
Clap hands, slap hands, jump in the air!
I'm having a party! See you there!

—Susan Moger

177 Beautiful Soup

Beautiful Soup, so rich and green,
Waiting in a hot **tureen**!
Who for such **dainties** would not stoop?
Soup of the evening, beautiful Soup!
Soup of the evening, beautiful Soup!

    Beau—ootiful Soo-oop!
    Beau—ootiful Soo-oop!
Soo—oop of the e—e—evening,
    Beautiful, beautiful Soup!

Beautiful Soup! Who cares for fish,
Game, or any other dish?
Who would not give all else for two
Pennyworth only of Beautiful Soup?
Pennyworth only of beautiful Soup?

    Beau—ootiful Soo-oop!
    Beau—ootiful Soo-oop!
Soo—oop of the e—e—evening,
    Beautiful, beauti—FUL SOUP!

—Lewis Carroll

Key Vocabulary

tureen: large soup bowl
dainties: delicious treats
pennyworth: something worth a penny, therefore, a small amount

Springboard

Invite students to perform this as a choral reading with different voices reading the chorus and stanzas.

178 A Fly and a Flea in a Flue

A Fly and a Flea in a **Flue**
Were imprisoned, so what could they do?
Said the fly, "Let us **flee**!"
"Let us fly!" said the flea.
So they flew through a flaw in the flue.

—Anonymous

Key Vocabulary

flue: the inside of a chimney
flee: run away

179 Three Plum Buns

Three plum buns
To eat here at the **stile**
In the clover meadow,
For we have walked a mile.
One for you, and one for me,
And one left over:
Give it to the boy who shouts
To scare sheep from the clover.

—Christina Rossetti

 Key Vocabulary

stile: steps over a
    fence or hedge

180 Look and See

Suddenly the world's in focus:
Plain as day
I can read the sign across the street
And find my way.
A bumblebee, your face, my book
Are there to see, if I just look.
Hello, blue sea and waving grasses,
I can see you now—
I found my glasses!

—Susan Moger

181 Drake

There once was a **drake**
Named Jake
Who went in a lake
With a snow flake
(I think it melted.)

—Roy Moger-Reischer

 Key Vocabulary

drake: male duck

182 # Up the Hill

              the hill
           Up
        Up
    Up

I won't
        I will
I won't
        I will

I won't
won't
won't

        I will
      will
      will
Make it

              the hill!
           Up
        Up
    Up

—Susan Moger

Springboard

Students can experiment with reciting this poem in different voices—high and low, loud and soft—but with each line ending on a triumphant note. Encourage children to write poems modeled on this one, in which the words are placed on the page in such a way as to suggest what the poem is saying.

183 # Mix a Pancake

Mix a pancake,
Stir a pancake,
Pop it in the pan;
Fry the pancake,
Toss the pancake,
Catch it if you can.

—Christina Rossetti

184 The Fairies (Excerpt)

. . . Up the airy mountain
Down the **rushy glen**,
    We daren't go a-hunting,
For fear of little men;
    Wee folk, good folk,
Trooping all together;
    Green jacket, red cap,
And white owl's feather.
    Down along the rocky shore
Some make their home,
    They live on crispy pancakes
Of yellow tide-foam;
    Some in the reeds
Of the black mountain-lake,
    With frogs for their watch-dogs,
All night awake.

—William Allingham

Key Vocabulary

rushy glen: grassy valley
wee folk: mythical small people
trooping: walking

185 The Jumblies (Excerpt)

. . . They went to sea in a **Sieve**, they did,
In a Sieve they went to sea:
    In spite of all their friends could say,
    On a winter's morn, on a stormy day,
In a Sieve they went to sea!
    And when the Sieve turned round and round,
    And every one cried, 'You'll all be drowned!'
    They called aloud, 'Our Sieve ain't big,
    But we don't care a button! we don't care a fig!
In a Sieve we'll go to sea!'

—Edward Lear

Key Vocabulary

sieve: a pot-size strainer

186

The Night Wind

Have you ever heard the wind go "Yooooo"?
　　'Tis a pitiful sound to hear!
It seems to chill you through and through
　　With a strange and speechless fear.
5　'Tis the voice of the night that **broods**
outside
　　When folk should be asleep,
And many and many's the time I've cried
To the darkness brooding far and wide
10　　Over the land and the **deep**:
"Whom do you want, O lonely night,
　　That you wail the long hours through?"
And the night would say in its ghostly way:
　　　　"Yoooooooo!
15　　　　Yoooooooo!
　　　　Yoooooooo!"
My mother told me long ago
　　(When I was a little **tad**)
That when the night went wailing so,
20　　Somebody had been bad;
And then, when I was snug in bed,
　　Whither I had been sent,
With the blankets pulled up round my head,
I'd think of what my mother'd said,
25　　And wonder what boy she meant!
And "Who's been bad to-day?" I'd ask
　　Of the wind that hoarsely blew,
And the voice would say in its meaningful
way:
30　　　　"Yoooooooo!
　　　　Yoooooooo!
　　　　Yoooooooo!"

That this was true I must allow—
　　You'll not believe it, though!
35　Yes, though I'm quite a model now,
　　I was not always so.
And if you doubt what things I say,
　　Suppose you make the test;
Suppose, when you've been bad some day
40　And up to bed are sent away
　　From mother and the rest—
Suppose you ask, "Who has been bad?"
　　And then you'll hear what's true;
For the wind will moan in its **ruefullest** tone:
45　　　　"Yoooooooo!
　　　　Yoooooooo!
　　　　Yoooooooo!"

—Eugene Field

Key
Vocabulary

'tis: it is
broods: thinks deeply about
deep: the sea
tad: child, from *tadpole*
whither: where
ruefullest: most regretful

Read aloud
with gusto!